Taxation in Ireland:
An Economist's Perspective

TAXATION IN IRELAND:
AN ECONOMIST'S PERSPECTIVE

John Bristow

IPA

INSTITUTE OF PUBLIC
ADMINISTRATION

First Published 2004
by the Institute of Public Administration
57-61 Lansdowne Road
Dublin 4
Ireland

ISBN 1 904541 05 4

British Library Cataloguing in Publication Data
A catalogue record for this book is available from the British Library

Cover design by M. and J. Graphics Ltd, Dublin
Origination by Carole Lynch, Sligo
Printed in Ireland by Betaprint, Dublin

Contents

Preface   vii

1   The Structure of Tax Revenue   1
2   The Economic Approach to Tax Policy   7
3   The Taxation of Income and Capital Gains   37
4   The Taxation of Wealth   85
5   The Taxation of Consumption   99
6   Conclusions   115

Appendix: The Incidence of VAT   125
Further Reading   133
Index   134

Preface

Tax reform is a dominant slogan in Irish politics. One of its major themes originated as long ago as the late 1950s, when it was decided to use corporate tax incentives as part of a package to change the whole strategy of development policy. Ireland was perhaps the first developing country to move the basis of that policy from protection and import-substitution to the promotion of exports and inward investment; the two being intimately linked since it was expected that foreign investors would bring with them markets as well as capital. The main tax component of this package was to grant tax-free status to profits earned on manufacturing exports. This sectoral concession had to be abolished when Ireland joined the European Economic Community in 1973. The Community disapproved of this as a form of export-subsidisation and it was replaced in a phased manner by an extremely low nominal corporate tax rate which would eventually apply to all corporate profits.

The next important episode for the Irish tax system began during the 1970s with general dissatisfaction with income tax and culminated in massive public demonstrations in 1979. The government responded by setting up a Commission on Taxation, which produced, in the form of a series of reports published between 1982 and 1985, the most thorough and wide-ranging analysis of the Irish tax system yet seen. Several of its recommendations were eventually implemented, but, despite some quite significant structural reforms, there is still a tendency on the part of Irish politicians and the general public to regard tax reform as primarily referring to reductions in *rates* of tax (especially of income taxes), with structural issues being given less importance. We here reverse this emphasis.

This book is designed for readers interested in tax policy but with little knowledge of economics. It is, therefore, non-technical and devoid of the normal academic apparatus of references to the literature. After an introductory chapter displaying some quantitative information on the structure of the Irish tax system, Chapter 2 sets out the basics of the conceptual framework traditionally employed in economic tax analysis and forms the foundation of the rest of the book. That chapter, and indeed the work as a whole, gives more prominence to issues of equity and administrative simplicity than the writings of most economists, whose work is traditionally dominated by concerns for economic efficiency. The stress on equity derives from the view that taxation is fundamental to a citizen's relationships with government; the fact that tax laws are as coercive as other laws and so should obey the canons we prescribe for all laws – above all that they be manifestly fair; and the belief that inequity reduces public respect for tax law. Administrative simplicity is desirable, not only to minimise waste in the use of resources needed to collect taxes, but also because complexity breeds inequity as those who can afford professional advice can take greater advantage of complexity than those who cannot.

The remainder of the book applies these concepts to the main parts of the Irish tax system. Chapter 3 deals with the taxation of income, including capital gains tax and social security taxes. Formally, social security taxes (called social welfare contributions in Ireland) are separate, but they are, in their application and effect, essentially an adjunct to income tax – so much so that it makes little sense to ignore them when looking at the taxation of labour incomes.

Chapter 4 reviews the issues relating to the taxation of wealth. In Ireland, the only central taxes using assets (rather than income from assets) as the base are: a capital transfer tax called capital acquisitions tax, and stamp duties applying to the transfer of documents relating to the ownership of certain assets. There is also a business property tax (rates) operated at the level of local government, but this is ignored here.

The taxation of consumption through value-added tax (VAT) and selective excises is discussed in Chapter 5. Taxes from which relatively little revenue is raised are referred to in passing throughout the book where appropriate. The final chapter summarises the conclusions drawn in the preceding chapters and looks ahead at possible pressures from the European Union to change Irish taxes.

In the absence of reasonably elegant gender-neutral singular personal pronouns, I adopt the traditional usage of he/him/his when gender is irrelevant and I hope that any reader offended by this will forgive me for choosing simplicity over equity on this occasion.

This is intended as an economist's review of the tax system and not as a guide for taxpayers seeking to order their affairs. I accept no responsibility for any loss suffered by any person acting or refraining from acting as a result of the material in this book. Professional advice should always be sought before acting on a tax issue.

I owe special debts to Becky Bristow and Donal de Buitleir, who read the whole manuscript and rescued me from many sins of omission and commission. Those remaining are entirely my responsibility, especially since I often chose to ignore their advice. My thanks also go to Jennifer Armstrong for the skill and tact with which she managed the publication process.

The tax provisions discussed here are those ruling in 2003.

J.A.B.

1

The Structure of Tax Revenue

We begin with an overview, in terms of revenue, of the size and structure of the Irish tax system, placing it in an international context. Table 1.1 shows how total revenue has changed in relation to GDP since 1970.

Table 1.1: Total tax revenue (% of GDP)

	1970	1980	1990	2000
Ireland	29.9	31.4	33.5	31.1
Total OECD*	28.8	32.1	35.1	37.4
Total EU 15*	30.9	35.7	39.5	41.6

* Unweighted average

Source: OECD, *Revenue Statistics: 1965/2001*, Paris: OECD, 2002

Table 1.1 gives the lie to the idea that Ireland is heavily taxed by the standards of the developed world. Ireland is one of the very few OECD countries whose tax/GDP ratio declined between 1990 and 2000 and which has had a ratio lower than the averages for both the OECD and the EU since 1970. In 2000, only four of the thirty OECD members had a ratio less than Ireland's, and none of those is in Europe.

In recent times, there has been some debate as to whether or not this low ratio is a statistical mirage. It has been argued that GDP is the wrong denominator and that GNP would be more appropriate as a measure of taxable capacity.[1] This point relies on the fact that Ireland is unusual in that its GDP is almost 20 per cent higher than its GNP, whereas in most countries these magnitudes are more equal. As a result, tax as a proportion of GNP is very similar in Ireland to the equivalent ratio in other developed countries. Be that as it may, it is not at all clear why anyone should claim that GNP is the more appropriate measure of taxable capacity. It is universal practice for countries to tax income generated domestically, regardless of the residence of the recipient. Thus, profits generated in Ireland are taxable in Ireland, even if they are subsequently repatriated abroad. Such repatriated profits, part of GDP but not of GNP, are legitimately part of Ireland's tax base. So, there are good reasons for comparing tax/GDP ratios when judging whether a country effectively taps into its potential tax base.

Table 1.2 shows the evolution of tax structures between 1970 and 2000. In 1970, the composition of Ireland's tax revenue was markedly different from that of the typical developed country: a mere 27 per cent coming from income taxes, a massive 52 per cent from consumption taxes and only 8 per cent from social security contributions, compared with OECD averages of 36, 36 and 20 per cent respectively.[2]

Since 1980, Ireland's tax structure has, with two exceptions, noticeably converged towards the norm. The first exception is the explosion in the importance of corporate income tax in the 1990s, whereas this item changed relatively little in the OECD as a whole. This happened despite the unusually low rate of corporation tax in Ireland and is explained by the very rapid growth of corporate profits in that period. Of more long-term interest is the fact that the proportion of total revenue accounted for by social security contributions in Ireland has remained at only half of that typical within the OECD and the EU. In most EU countries, contributions account for over 30 per cent of revenue and in only three members – Ireland, the UK and Denmark – does the proportion fall below 20 per cent. Denmark is a special

---

1   Gross domestic product (GDP) is a measure of the total income generated within the country, whereas gross national product (GNP) is a measure of the total income received by the residents of the country. The difference is net factor income from abroad, which, for Ireland, is significantly negative because of the large volume of profits generated here that are abroad.

2   The huge decline in the importance of wealth taxes in Ireland in the 1970s (leading to Ireland's figures becoming more typical) was the result of the abolition of estate duties and their replacement with a capital acquisitions tax with such high exemption levels that revenue collapsed.

Table 1.2: Structure of tax revenue (% of total tax revenue)

	1970	1980	1990	2000
Personal income[a]				
Ireland	18.3	32.0	31.9	30.8
Total OECD*	27.9	31.3	29.3	26.0
Total EU 15*	25.4	29.0	27.1	25.6
Corporate income[b]				
Ireland	8.8	4.5	5.0	12.1
Total OECD*	8.8	7.6	7.9	9.7
Total EU 15*	6.9	5.8	6.8	9.2
Consumption[c]				
Ireland	52.4	43.7	42.3	37.2
Total OECD*	35.6	32.3	31.9	31.6
Total EU 15*	36.1	31.0	31.6	30.0
Social security				
Ireland	8.2	14.3	14.8	13.6
Total OECD*	19.5	22.2	22.7	24.5
Total EU 15*	24.4	28.9	28.1	27.5
Wealth[d]				
Ireland	12.2	5.3	4.7	5.6
Total OECD*	7.1	5.3	5.7	5.4
Total EU 15*	5.8	4.2	4.3	5.0

* Unweighted average

[a] Taxes on income and capital gains not accruing to companies

[b] Taxes on income and capital gains accruing to companies

[c] VAT and other general sales taxes, excises and customs duties

[d] Wealth taxes, capital transfer taxes and stamp duties

Source: OECD, *Revenue Statistics: 1965/2001*, Paris: OECD, 2002

case in that its social security system is funded primarily from personal income taxes rather than separate social security taxes.[3] The main reason why social security taxes are, relatively, of such low importance in Ireland

---

3   In Denmark, over 50 per cent of tax revenue comes from personal income taxes. When this is added to the remarkably low 4 per cent accounted for by social security taxes, that country is very close to the EU norm.

and the UK is that the dominant element of social security expenditure – public pensions – is much lower than is typical in the rest of the EU.[4]

To end this description of revenue structure, Tables 1.3 and 1.4 present some more detailed data on the produce of the various Irish taxes for the recent past.[5] The patterns revealed by these tables reflect two major factors: rapid growth of income, consumption and wealth (and, therefore, in the bases of all taxes) in the era of the Celtic Tiger; and significant reductions in nominal and effective rates of income taxes. Thus, the figures in Table 1.3 reflect the following circumstances:

- excise duties declined in importance because specific rates[6] failed to keep pace with inflation
- VAT increased in importance because the rates did not change in the face of a rapid increase in the base of this tax (taxable consumption)
- corporation tax increased in importance, reflecting the explosion in corporate income and the termination of certain especially favourable capital allowances such as free depreciation
- income tax declined in importance, despite the rapid increase in the base, because of substantial reductions in effective tax rates
- social welfare contributions declined in importance because the base (wages and salaries) declined relative to other forms of income and because effective rates declined[7]
- stamp duties became somewhat more important – a reflection of the substantial increase in the value of those assets that attract stamp duty when traded
- capital gains tax markedly increased its relative contribution, despite a dramatic reduction in the nominal rate from 40 to 20 per cent, because the base of the tax exploded as a result of the very significant increase in

---

4   In Ireland and the UK, public pensions are fixed sums, whereas in most other EU member states – and, indeed, in many other OECD members – they are related to pre-retirement earnings. Also, private pension provision is relatively more significant in Ireland.

5   The totals in these tables fall slightly short of those in Tables 1.1 and 1.2 because they exclude the very low-yielding property taxes levied by local authorities.

6   Excise duties come in two forms: some are *specific*, where the tax rate is €x per unit of volume; and others are *ad valorem*, where the tax rate is x per cent of the value at the point where the excise is applied.

7   The ceiling, above which the marginal rate of contribution is zero, was not adjusted sufficiently in the face of increasing average wages and increased skewness in the distribution of labour incomes.

asset values. The reduction in the rate may also have encouraged holders to release assets, especially since the reduction was originally stated to be temporary and the rate would, after a few years, be raised to 60 per cent. At the time of writing, this increase has yet to happen.

Table 1.3: Ireland: Net tax revenue by type of tax* (% of total)

	1996	1997	1998	1999	2000
Customs duties	1.1	1.1	0.9	0.7	0.7
Excise duties	16.2	15.4 1	5.2	14.8	14.0
Value-added tax	21.8	22.7	23.0	22.8	23.6
Capital acquisitions tax	0.6	0.5	0.6	0.7	0.7
Capital gains tax	0.6	0.8	1.0	1.7	2.4
Stamp duties	2.3	2.6	2.9	3.4	3.4
Residential property tax	–	–	–	–	–
Corporation tax	10.0	10.4	11.1	12.6	12.3
Income tax	32.1	31.9	31.0	29.4	28.9
Social welfare contributions	15.2	14.5	14.3	14.0	13.9

* Gross revenue less adjustments for previous over-payments, refunds to non-liable persons of tax withheld at source, tax credits on corporate distributions, and VAT refunds

Source: Office of the Revenue Commissioners, *Statistical Report 2001,* Dublin: Government Publications, 2002

It can be seen from Table 1.4 that, as a result of all the above factors, there was almost no change in the relative importance of consumption taxes, but a marked change in the incidence of income taxes. Taxes on labour income (wages) fell from 31 to 26 per cent of the total, whereas those on business and capital income (profits, interest and capital gains) increased from 27 to 32 per cent of the total.[8]

---

8   These figures probably slightly overstate the shift away from labour taxes because an unknown proportion of business taxes (those on unincorporated businesses) is based on what are in effect the salaries of proprietors.

Table 1.4: Ireland: Net tax revenue by type of base (% of total)

	1996	1997	1998	1999	2000
Consumption[a]	38.0	38.1	38.2	37.6	37.6
Labour income[b]	31.1	30.3	29.2	27.9	25.9
Business income[c]	25.3	25.6	26.1	27.4	27.3
Other income[d]	1.5	1.7	2.1	2.4	4.3
Other taxes[e]	4.1	4.3	4.4	4.7	4.8

[a] VAT and excise duties

[b] PAYE and employees' social welfare contributions (assumed to be one-quarter of total)

[c] Corporation tax, business income tax, and employers' social welfare contributions (assumed to be three-quarters of total)

[d] Deposit interest retention tax, dividend withholding tax, capital gains tax and income levy

[e] Customs duties, stamp duties, residential property tax and capital acquisitions tax

2

The Economic Approach to Tax Policy

Almost everyone has views about taxation. The annual Budget programmes on television and radio attract large audiences and the newspapers provide multi-page coverage of the tax changes proposed by the Minister for Finance. Of course, for many people, the main focus of attention is on how their income tax bill will change or how VAT alterations will affect their cost of living. But even that focus shows signs of broadening: people worry about the standard of public services and increasingly accept that low taxation and high public expenditures are incompatible in the long run. Interest groups are concerned only to lobby for reductions in the tax bills of their members, usually arguing that the public interest will be served by such reductions. Politicians know how important tax policy is to most voters and, especially if an election is imminent, shy away from changes that would adversely affect the interests of a significant constituency.

Taxation is also of concern to several groups of professionals – notably lawyers, accountants and the specialised hybrid called tax consultants. In their everyday work, these advisors must understand the technical details of the regime so that they can ensure compliance on the part of their clients or can effectively advise on methods of minimising tax bills. Nonetheless, lawyers and accountants, especially of the academic kind, have contributed a great deal to the analysis of tax systems; and the judiciary has contributed some very significant judgments, which in some cases have been incorporated into legislation.[1]

---

1   For example, the taxation of married couples changed dramatically in 1980 as a result of a Supreme Court decision.

This book reflects the approach to taxation of another group of professionals: economists. In its emphasis anyway, the economist's approach tends to be different from that taken by, for instance, the lawyer, and the major purpose of this chapter is to review the way the economics profession has traditionally evaluated tax systems – that is, to set out what could be called the conceptual framework typically adopted in economic tax analysis. But before embarking on that task, an important point should be made. Some economists are concerned with the overall level of taxation (often portrayed as tax revenue as a proportion of, say, gross domestic product), believing that this has macroeconomic significance or, in a few cases, a significance for such matters as individual freedom. Such concerns are not addressed here. Instead, the revenue required to be raised by taxes is taken as given and what is at issue is the way that revenue is generated. That is, the focus here is the *structure* of Ireland's tax system and, in particular, the structure of the individual taxes. It is important to make this point because there is a widespread view, encouraged by successive Ministers for Finance, that a mere reduction in nominal tax rates represents tax reform, which in a sense it does, but that is not the sense employed here.

Any normative approach to taxation must be based on a set of criteria or principles, according to which taxes are to be judged. In the case of lawyers and accountants, clarity, certainty, consistency with other laws (and especially with the Constitution) and measurability are paramount considerations. Economists, of course, accept these as relevant criteria (after all, certainty was explicitly adopted as a tax criterion by the grandfather of the economics profession, Adam Smith), but require a lot more from a good tax system. They put at the centre of their concerns something that is uniquely economic and, indeed, barely comprehensible to non-economists: economic efficiency.

However, before reviewing the way economists typically evaluate tax systems, it is necessary to understand the concept of incidence.

Tax incidence

Incidence is concerned with the location of the burden of taxation and comes in two forms. First, the law defines who is liable for tax – that is, who sends the cheque to the collector-general and who can be pursued on default. This is called formal incidence. Second, the person bearing the formal incidence is almost certain to adjust his behaviour in an effort to restore his post-tax income. An obvious example would be a shopkeeper who pays VAT (few final consumers pay VAT in the formal sense) raising his prices to cover at least some of the liability. This process is usually called tax shifting and the resulting pattern of reduction in disposable income is called effective incidence. This is so important that more needs to be said about it.

The traditional view of effective incidence is oddly inconsistent. We sometimes call things like VAT and excises 'indirect' taxes; and things like income tax 'direct' taxes – reflecting an expectation that the former will be shifted but the latter will not. Indeed, Ministers for Finance usually say that a proposed increase in excise duties will mean so many cents on the retail price of a packet of cigarettes or a pint of beer, but they never say that a proposed increase in income tax or corporation tax means so much on the average wage or the average prices charged by companies. This is strange. An income tax on wages is a sales tax on labour supply and is in principle shiftable in exactly the same way as VAT or a tax on corporate profits.

What is more, shifting can take place in either direction. Parties to economic transactions are typically both sellers and buyers. A worker is a seller of labour and a buyer of goods, whereas a firm is a seller of goods and a buyer of other goods and of the services of labour (and of capital and land). If you bear a tax on your income (like a worker paying income tax on his wages or a shopkeeper paying VAT on his sales), you may adjust your selling or buying behaviour, or both. If you change your buying behaviour, you are engaging in backward shifting (a worker, because of the wages tax, spends less on goods and so reduces the income of shopkeepers; or a company, because of the corporation tax, reduces wages and/or employment). If you change your selling behaviour, you are engaging in forward shifting (a worker works less overtime or a shopkeeper increases his prices).

As a result of these tax-induced changes in behaviour, the pattern of effective incidence may be markedly different from that of formal incidence and would usually be complex to trace in any detail. However, at the qualitative level, we do know that the extent of shifting will depend upon the price-elasticities of demand for and supply of goods, services and factors of production.[2] These in turn will depend upon preferences and

---

2   The price-elasicity of demand or supply is a measure of the extent to which the amount people want to buy or sell, respectively, responds to a change in price.

market power, the latter sometimes affected by institutional rigidities. The following example illustrates these points.

Suppose the general rate of VAT is increased. How does the seller respond? There is a general assumption that the prices of all taxable goods will increase by the amount of the extra VAT – but why should this be? If the pre-VAT price is €100 and the VAT rate is raised from 10 to 20 per cent, we are expecting that the price in the shop will go from €110 to €120. But if the seller can get a price of €120 with no effect on the volume of sales, why did he not charge that price initially? The key lies in the qualification 'with no effect on the volume of sales'. If the seller is in a strong market position (such that the buyer has no convenient alternative source of supply), then he may have restricted his initial ambitions for fear of attracting either competitors or the attentions of the Competition Authority. If the seller is in a strongly competitive environment, he would not have been able to charge the high price initially and may, indeed, choose to bear some of the extra VAT himself to avoid losing market share. Even the most casual observer will have noted how, on occasion, supermarkets advertise that they will pay part of the VAT.

In general, for goods and services supplied in a reasonably competitive market, the VAT will not be fully shifted forward: some of it may be shifted backward (the higher prices may lead to a fall in volume and the seller will buy less from his suppliers and may hire less labour or no longer offer overtime working) and some of it will remain in the form of a reduction in the seller's profits.

Prices will almost certainly increase to some extent, but that is not the end of the story. The VAT increase has raised the price of consumption and the population at large may respond in one or more of five ways:

- they may consume less in nominal terms – that is, save more
- they may save less in an effort to protect their real standard of consumption
- they may change their pattern of consumption because not all prices will rise to the same extent due to differences among goods in the application of the general rate and in the incentive or opportunity for forward shifting
- they may work less – that is, shift their consumption to something that the VAT cannot be applied to, which is leisure

- they may attempt to increase their income, perhaps by looking for an increase in wages.

These ripple effects are very difficult to trace in detail, and little of such work has been done in Ireland. But, as already noted, we can make qualitative statements. Above all, we must ask what kind of behavioural response is likely, as opposed to conceivable. Noting that any tax change causes, somewhere, a change in relative prices, and must, if it is to change revenue, cause someone's disposable income to change, we then have to consider the extent to which buying and selling behaviour is in fact adjustable. For simplicity, only a few of the possibilities are considered below.

Will a general increase in consumer prices cause people to save more or save less? Given their income, this will depend upon how important it is to consume rather than save. Thus, a family with small children will probably save less because it is important to them to maintain their level of consumption, whereas a middle-aged single person with an eye to the future may give up some of his more luxurious consumption so as to protect his pension position. In general, it rather depends upon whether or not the person is locked into a savings scheme that makes it impossible or very expensive to reduce the level of saving.

Will the inevitably non-uniform pattern of price changes cause consumption to shift towards goods and services whose price has increased less? This depends on consumer preferences. We know, for instance, that the price-elasticity of demand for tobacco is very low, at least in the short run. Similarly with energy (petroleum products and electricity), which is not a separate final good and has to be used with equipment that cannot be changed in the short run. So, if there is an above-average rise in the prices of such items, an increased proportion of a household's budget is likely to go on these items and there will be expenditure-switching at the expense of those goods where the price-elasticity of demand is higher. Since real disposable income has changed, consumption patterns will also change because, typically, those with different incomes have different consumption patterns. Expenditure is likely to shift away from the kind of things one can afford only when one is relatively affluent. Furthermore, an increase in the general price of consumption goods may cause people to work less and to increase their consumption of leisure instead. The opportunities for this depend on the flexibility of the institutional environment in which workers find themselves and the extent to which they can vary their hours of work. For instance, we know that the willingness to work overtime is influenced by the marginal rate of income tax, as is the willingness of people to enter the formal labour force at all.

In addition to these channels of shifting, it is possible that people may be able to respond to a tax-induced increase in prices by increasing their income. It is well known that centralised pay bargaining, in the form of national partnership agreements, reflects the ability of trade unions to influence labour supply. An agreement to restrain demands for increases in gross wages is purchased by an agreement to reduce income tax. This is another reflection of the general point that the greater the market power of the person who bears the formal incidence the more likely shifting is to occur.

Changes in behaviour in response to taxes can lead to unexpected effects, as illustrated by the following two examples. The first is the possibility that a reduction in the stamp duty on the conveyancing of real property will *increase* the market price of such property. Suppose a house sells for €200,000 and there is a stamp duty of 10 per cent imposed on the buyer. Now suppose that the duty had not existed. The buyer was prepared to pay a total of €220,000 and the seller knows this. In the absence of the duty, he would therefore charge €220,000, the buyer would happily pay this and the sale would take place. All that has happened is that the sum paid by the buyer is no longer shared between the seller and the government. The market price has risen by the amount of the now non-existent stamp duty. It will also be noted that, for a given revenue (€20,000), it makes no difference whether the formal incidence of the stamp duty is on the buyer or the seller. If it falls on the seller, the market price is €220,000 and the rate of duty is 9.1 per cent: he gets a net €200,000 of the total €220,000 that the buyer pays. If it falls on the buyer, the rate of duty is 10 per cent and, again, the seller gets €200,000 of the total amount paid by the buyer. Whatever the formal incidence, the buyer pays and the seller receives the same amount.

The second example illustrates the phenomenon of tax capitalisation. Suppose there is a tax on the ownership of real property (such as local authority rates). When deciding how much he is prepared to pay for a property, a potential buyer takes the tax into account. If the tax were abolished, he would be prepared to pay more. The market will therefore drive the price up. The result is a windfall gain for those who owned property at the time of the abolition of the tax: those who subsequently buy property gain nothing from the abolition of the tax. This idea that a tax is capitalised into the value of an asset has important implications for wealth/property taxation and for the taxation of income from capital.

Tax shifting occurs as a result of behaviour being changed by taxes and so is of great importance in evaluating policy proposals, if only because there is a widespread tendency to ignore it and to believe that effective incidence coincides with formal incidence (which is the same as believing that taxes do not affect behaviour). This is odd, especially in a country like Ireland, whose tax system is riddled with non-uniformity, much of which makes no sense unless it is believed that taxes influence behaviour. No analysis of tax policy can be effective unless shifting – the result of changes in behaviour in response to tax changes – is taken into account.

Progressive, proportional and regressive taxes

Discussion of taxation, especially when it comes to matters of equity, uses the terms progressive, proportional and regressive. It is essential to have agreement on the definition of these terms. To take income tax as an example, the tax is progressive if as gross (or, in some contexts, taxable) income rises, the proportion of that income payable in tax (the average or effective rate) rises.[3] If the average rate is constant as income rises, the tax is proportional. If the average rate falls as income rises, the tax is regressive.

It will be noted that, to be progressive, an income tax does not need the stepped system of marginal rates familiar in most countries (in Ireland, there are two non-zero marginal rates). A single marginal rate combined with the exemption of the first slice of income (say, a personal allowance) will cause the average rate to rise as income rises because an increasing proportion of income is taxed at the single, marginal rate (or, looking at it the other way, the exemption covers a decreasing proportion of income).

One has to be careful with taxes whose base is other than income, such as VAT or excises, because, in popular debate, labels like progressive or

---

3   The marginal rate is the rate applied to an additional euro of income, whereas the average rate is the rate on total income.

regressive tend to be used to refer to the way tax as a proportion of *income* changes as income changes, rather than what happens to tax as a proportion of the *tax base* as that base changes. Thus, even a completely universal and uniform VAT, whose base is not income but total consumption, is often called regressive because the ratio of total consumption to income tends to fall as income rises, and so VAT payments as a proportion of income fall as income rises. To avoid confusion, I shall use expressions like progressive or regressive 'with respect to the tax base' or 'with respect to income', where the context permits ambiguity.

The three main criteria that traditionally provide the foundation of economic tax analysis are: economic efficiency, equity (or justice or fairness) and administrative efficiency, and these are now reviewed.

ECONOMIC EFFICIENCY

At the very core of economics is the concept of scarcity of available resources. 'Resources' is a very broad notion covering everything that goes into the production of goods and services: labour force, stock of capital, natural resources, knowledge about productive techniques and so on. At any point in time, the volume of production is constrained by the volume of available resources; and, over time, the rate of real growth in an economy is limited by the rate at which the volume of resources grows. Economic efficiency relates to the extent to which a society manages to get the most out of the resources available to it and the policy challenge is to find the structure of mechanisms that permits this to happen. The basic conclusion is that, except in certain circumstances, voluntary market interaction between buyers and sellers will maximise their own welfare, and hence the welfare of society, and that government policies should interfere as little as possible with that voluntary interaction.

It must be stressed that the economist's predilection for the outcomes generated by market mechanisms is not ideological in the normal sense. It is the end-point of a reasoning process that appeals primarily to two assertions: a person left to his own devices will make decisions that improve his own welfare, and society is better off if its individual members are better off.

There are exceptions to the conclusion that free markets enable society to get the best out of its resources; or, to put it another way, this conclusion is valid only if certain conditions are satisfied. In very broad terms, the relevant exceptions are as follows. First, some markets may be very uncompetitive in that either sellers or buyers have significant monopoly power. This enables the seller to charge prices in excess of the true costs of production – that is the costs which reflect the scarcity of the resources used in producing what is traded – or, if it is the buyer who has the market power, forces the seller to charge prices which fall short of those costs. Few markets are sufficiently competitive to escape this exception completely. However, it would be rare for tax policy to be the best instrument for dealing with these problems – competition laws are better – and so it would be usual for taxes to be framed on the assumption that the relevant markets are at least reasonably competitive. An exception to this general case may be the exploitation of minerals (including oil and gas) and it is no coincidence that mineral taxation is often different from the taxation of other activities.

Second, markets can fail to generate desirable outcomes if there are significant externalities associated with the production or consumption of a good or service – that is, production or consumption adversely or beneficially affects those other than the producer or consumer of the good or service. Examples include traffic congestion and environmental pollution (negative externalities: others suffer), primary education and vaccination against contagious diseases (positive externalities: others benefit). Tax policy can certainly be relevant in dealing with negative externalities, as exemplified by topical debates over pollution taxes or tobacco excises. Positive externalities may be recognised through the especially favourable tax treatment of relevant activities, although it is more often the expenditure side of the Budget that is used in this context. However, before appealing to externalities to justify special tax measures, they must be well identified. Just because something is regarded as good does not mean that there is an externality; this is the case with special favours to owner-occupiers of houses on the grounds that owner-occupation is somehow beneficial to society at large.

The third main cause of market failure is that buyers or sellers may not have complete information about what is to be traded or about other opportunities available to them. Tax favours may be granted, not merely to encourage people to behave in a certain way, but to encourage them to even consider, say, an investment (perhaps in central Dublin or tourist accommodation). While the assumption that traders have complete information is fundamental to the case for leaving markets unconstrained, it is far from obvious that tax policy is an appropriate response if that assumption is violated. It would surely be more relevant for the authorities to provide the missing information, although sometimes a tax concession may induce an investor to investigate an opportunity that may otherwise be overlooked.

Markets operate through a network of signals giving information as to the desires of buyers and the costs of sellers, the latter reflecting the scarcity of the resources employed in the production of the good or service being traded. By far the most important of these signals is price and so economists usually regard the efficiency criterion as meaning that, for a given revenue, taxes should be designed so as to minimise their impact on market prices (for factors of production as well as goods and services). That is, taxes should be neutral in the sense of not affecting consumption, investment and production decisions – they should not distort the prices upon which those decisions are based. This may not be the overriding criterion in any particular case, but an efficient tax is one that interferes as little as possible with market behaviour. The central implication of this is that we need to have a well-identified example of market failure if we are to support tax policies explicitly designed to influence behaviour. Since the Irish system is riddled with tax concessions designed to influence behaviour, this issue arises frequently.

Of course, all taxes interfere with market behaviour because they extract purchasing power from taxpayers: they have what the jargon calls an income effect. But what creates economic inefficiency is not an income effect, but a substitution effect. This results from the fact that almost all taxes change relative prices or returns to factors of production. Even an entirely uniform VAT changes the relative prices of consumption and saving and the price of traded consumption goods relative to the price of leisure, which cannot be directly taxed but which is a good. Non-uniform taxes such as Ireland's VAT, which imposes different rates on different forms of consumption, and income taxes, which exempt income from certain sources, are replete with substitution effects.

It is through effects on relative prices and returns to factors of production that taxes affect economic behaviour. No price or return is high or low in absolute terms. When deciding to buy one brand rather than another, or choosing to work more rather than take more leisure, or investing in one asset rather than another, what we concentrate on, other things being equal, is the price or net-of-tax return relative to the available alternatives. Thus, if the tax system changes relative prices and returns, it distorts the key signals that determine our behaviour. The efficiency criterion asks whether or not this interference with market signals can be justified on the grounds that the resulting change in behaviour is socially beneficial. The baseline is the assumption that, other than in the circumstances summarised above, the behaviour resulting from undistorted market signals is the best we can do, and so there is a presumption in favour of tax neutrality. Only if we have good reasons to believe that, in a well-identified case, the signals generated by the market lead to behaviour which is less than optimal, would efficiency require a non-neutral tax regime.[4]

But what does a neutral tax look like and does it, for example, mean that consumption taxes such as VAT should be uniform in their formal incidence – that is, apply the same rate to all relevant transactions? In principle, the answer has to be negative. Some changes in relative prices have little effect on behaviour: substitution effects are low. Thus, if we apply a high VAT rate to goods for which there are few practicable substitutes – that is, for which the price-elasticity of demand is low – there will be little change in behaviour. On the other hand, a high rate on goods that have a high price-elasticity of demand will change behaviour. This suggests that VAT should not be uniform: the required rate should be inversely related to the elasticity of demand. Similar conditions apply to taxes on incomes: there should be higher rates on sources of income that respond little to variations in the net return. An example would be the claim that income from capital should be taxed less heavily than income from labour because capital is more mobile than labour – that is, taxes on capital income are more likely to change behaviour than taxes on labour income.

This kind of inverse-elasticity rule would clearly lead to outcomes we may, on other grounds, regard as undesirable. When applied to

---

4   The extent to which society is made worse off by tax-induced distortions in market signals and, therefore, in the allocation of resources is technically known as the excess burden of a tax. Efforts have been made to measure the scale of this burden and, in some cases, it has been estimated to amount to as much as 30 per cent of the value of the revenue from the tax.

consumption taxes, the rule would prescribe high rates on things like salt and toilet paper (because their price-elasticities of demand are low), whereas restaurant meals would have low rates (because their price-elasticities are high). This is exactly the opposite of what we observe in systems with non-uniform commodity taxes. The reason why we may dislike such non-uniformity is distributional. Goods with low price-elasticities of demand tend to be more necessitous and those with high price-elasticities more luxurious. So, in the interest of vertical equity (see below), higher rates tend to be placed on goods with higher elasticities of demand. Similarly with income taxes: the average recipient of capital income tends to be richer than the average wage-earner.

In practice, it would require an enormous amount of information to apply the inverse-elasticity rule with any precision. Furthermore, non-uniform taxes have markedly higher administrative costs than uniform taxes. So the difficulties in measuring relative elasticities, the fact that shifting is bound to be non-uniform and the increase in administrative costs associated with formally non-uniform taxes suggest that uniformity may be the best we can do.

Of course, economic efficiency – the search for taxes that minimise distortions to behaviour – is not the only criterion. One has only to look at why the British poll tax was rejected to see that there are other influences. Another criterion concerns equity (or justice or fairness) and we pass to that now.

HORIZONTAL EQUITY

Equity is a moral concept and, in a sense, economists have taken it over second-hand. Despite this, all the famous economists who have had something to say about taxation have placed importance on equity as a criterion of a good tax system, and many have adapted other philosophical concepts for economic purposes (or at least have translated those concepts into the language used by economists). It is typical to divide this concept into two parts – horizontal and vertical equity – and this dichotomy will be employed here.

The notion of horizontal equity can be summarised in the prescription that 'persons in equal situations should be treated equally' and this can be regarded as no more than a basic jurisprudential requirement that any law should be even-handed and not arbitrarily distinguish among those to whom the law is to be applied. Laws, of course, discriminate – convicted criminals are jailed, while (ideally) others are not – but we demand that any discrimination be based on justifiable distinctions. Thus, the severity of the crime may properly influence the sentence, but the colour of the criminal's hair may not. It must never be forgotten that taxes are enshrined in coercive laws and so we must apply the same even-handed criterion to taxes as we do to a criminal code. The following discussion is organised around the three questions arising from the prescription noted above. What is a person (or what is the tax unit)? How are equal situations to be identified? What does equal treatment mean?

The tax unit

All laws require a definition of 'person' so as to assign liability, but they differ according to how this atomic unit is to be defined. For some laws the relevant person is an individual (a natural person), but for others it is a group of individuals (a juridical, or legal, person). Thus, for most purposes, the law recognises a company as a person (it can enter into contracts, can breach regulatory laws, can incur tax liabilities, can be sued for torts, and so on). Partnerships can be parties to contracts or can incur certain tax liabilities (though not others), but would not be recognised as a legal person for many of the purposes for which incorporation creates a legal person. A similar situation applies with other groups such as clubs and, of particular importance in taxation, married couples (and, sometimes, their children).

In most cases where tax law employs a group definition of person, it simply takes over a definition established for more general legal purposes. Thus, the application of income tax to companies (often, as in Ireland, by means of a separate corporation tax) or to partnerships uses definitions based on a commercial code developed for much wider purposes. The particular significance for taxation of the individualistic versus group definition of person arises in the treatment of households under the personal income tax.

Although the situation is changing, in the past most income tax regimes employed a non-individualistic definition of the tax unit, either by grouping individuals together or by recognising a taxpayer's relationship to others in determining tax liability, or both. The first method aggregates the incomes of all group members in determining the tax base, whereas the second uses an essentially individualistic definition but provides standard deductions with respect to dependants in arriving at taxable income. The methods may be combined in a system which aggregates parental incomes and also gives allowances with respect to children or other dependent relatives. In recent times, many well-established tax systems have been moving towards a purer individualistic definition; the majority of newly independent countries, and formerly communist countries developing market-based tax systems, have used an individualistic definition from the outset.

The appropriate principles to guide the choice of tax unit involve a range of considerations going far beyond taxation. However, before venturing into those, let us be clear why it matters *financially*. All personal income taxes with which I am familiar are progressive, which means that the larger the taxable income, the higher the proportion of that income that is payable as income tax. Suppose that the effective rate on an income of €15,000 is 10 per cent and that on an income of €30,000 is 15 per cent. Take a married couple in which each spouse has an income of €15,000. If the tax unit is defined individualistically, each spouse pays €1,500 in tax and the couple pays total tax of €3,000. But suppose the couple is regarded as a single tax unit and so their incomes are aggregated in determining tax liability. Their aggregate income of €30,000 is subject to an effective rate of 15 per cent, which implies a total tax payment of €4,500, an increase of €1,500 on the previous case. Aggregation raises the effective tax rate on the total income of the couple, other things being equal. In addition, even the individualistic definition of the tax unit discriminates according to whether the total income is derived from one or two earners (€4,500 is payable if the €30,000 is earned by one spouse alone and €3,000 if it is earned in equal parts by the two spouses). This discrimination against single-income couples may be mitigated by giving the earning spouse a dependant's allowance with respect to the non-earning spouse or a tax credit that is larger than that provided for a single person.

So, the choice of tax unit makes a difference to total tax bills under a progressive tax. But there are other, and broader, issues at stake here. In the first place, the nature of the distinction between the alternative definitions depends critically upon which groups are accorded the non-individualistic definition (in our example, the members of which groups have their incomes aggregated). Thus, it was successfully argued before the Irish Supreme Court in 1980 that the system then in operation (essentially that in the above example) discriminated against married couples vis-à-vis cohabiting single persons. Should the tax system make such a discrimination?

Even broader is the matter of sex (or, if you insist, gender) discrimination. This issue arises for three main reasons. First, in some jurisdictions with aggregation, the husband files the joint return. This means that the husband has to know the wife's income, but not vice versa. Even without this discrimination, it has historically been the case that the husband is usually the major earner (or the only earner) and would typically make the return, again causing an inter-spouse asymmetry in information. Second, when both spouses are earning and file jointly, the lower earner will, under a progressive tax, face a higher marginal rate than would be the case if he were treated as an individual. This may be seen to be unfair and, in addition, large amounts of research show that it creates a disincentive to married women entering the formal labour force. Spouses treated jointly have to agree how deductions will be divided between them. If they cannot agree or do not express a wish in this matter, the tax authorities make the division and would always give most of the allowances to the major earner. It is, therefore, unlikely that the division of the deductions would be so much in favour of the lower earner as to reduce his marginal rate. Third, when an earning spouse receives an allowance with respect to a non-earning spouse, the non-earner is effectively labelled as a dependant, a status understandably regarded as demeaning, especially when this status arises because the couple have voluntarily engaged in a division of labour (one partner working outside the home, the other being a home-carer) that receives no recognition.[5]

The most fundamental argument for the individualistic definition comes from those who contend that people's household arrangements are simply no business of the tax law. If people marry and procreate, they should be assumed to do so voluntarily and foresee the financial consequences. If the group definition makes no difference to tax liability,

---

5   This egregious discrimination extends to the way we define employment and the way we measure national income.

it is a pointless invasion of privacy. If it makes a difference, it is discriminating on the basis of voluntary decisions (and intra-household sharing arrangements) that are no-one else's business. This very strong argument accounts for a worldwide movement towards the individualistic definition in personal income taxation. But there is a counter-argument.

In practice, married couples share income: if they did not, a non-earning spouse would starve. In effect, therefore, the apparently non-earning spouse has an income. One way the tax law could take account of this would be to assign part (arbitrarily, but reasonably, one-half) of the earning spouse's income to the non-earner and then apply an individualistic definition. This is called income-splitting and, in effect, is what the Irish tax law does for spouses who elect to be taxed jointly or for couples with only one earner. It still essentially involves the group definition, but merely to recognise de facto income-sharing. It does not appeal to any concept of dependence, but simply to a social fact. Its strengths are that it denies the degrading assumption made by national income accounting that house-spouses generate no product and so have no income, and recognises the very important fact that a couple with a given total income are worse off than an individual with that income.

Its weakness lies in the difficulty of restricting its application. If the argument stands for married couples, it stands for all household arrangements that involve income-sharing, among which would be unmarried couples and religious communities. Nonetheless, if the argument were to be found convincing in general terms, it could have practical application, even if the boundaries were somewhat arbitrary (but much less arbitrary than a system that restricts the benefits of the group definition to married couples). All that would be needed would be a definition of the stability of the relationship (for example, you can have the group definition applied to you in any tax year if you have lived together throughout the previous two years, or something like that).

Similar considerations apply to the question of whether dependent children should be included under any group definition.

Equal situations

Equal situations involve the equitable definition of the tax base. Despite the theoretical attractions of single-tax systems, all developed systems contain a multiplicity of taxes and so, to the extent that each tax is claimed to satisfy a requirement of horizontal equity, 'equal situations' have to be defined differently for each tax: that is, each tax has its own definition of the tax base. For consumption taxes such as VAT or excises, the definition is automatically implied by the nature of the tax. Two individuals are in equal situations if they consume the same combination of goods or, say, consume the same volume of cigarettes. It is in relation to income and capital taxes that more interesting issues arise.

The tax period

Let us initially dispose of an important, although rarely debated, issue. Any definition of income must include a specification of a time period, since income is a flow whose magnitude has no meaning without reference to a time period. Typically, tax systems define income in terms of a year.[6] In all countries not dominated by agriculture (or perhaps weather-dependent tourism), a year has no economic or social significance. However if income taxes are progressive, the time period makes a great difference to the effective rate of tax.

Take a system where the effective rate is 10 per cent on an income of €20,000 per year and 20 per cent on an income of €60,000 per year. Then take two individuals, each of whom earns €60,000 over a three-year period, the first earning this at a rate of €20,000 in each year and the second earning nothing in the first two years and the whole €60,000 in the third year. The former will pay, over the three years, tax of €6,000, whereas the latter will pay €12,000. Is this fair? Not obviously so, since the only difference between the two is the fact that the time profile of their incomes is different. An exactly equivalent example can be constructed where the tax period is a month and two individuals have equal incomes over a year, but this income is spread differently for the two persons.

The adoption of a year essentially says that multi-year differences in time profiles of income will affect tax liability, but multi-month differences will not. This is arbitrary and situations should be regarded as

---

6   Despite the fact that progressive withholding taxes on labour incomes (PAYE) operate on a weekly or monthly basis, these are usually administered so that, over a year, the correct amount of tax is deducted. The use of a year is universal in economically advanced countries, although a month is often used with respect to wages taxes in developing countries.

unequal only when their differences are not arbitrary. But what can be done about it, given that income has to be defined by reference to a time period? Essentially, there is no perfect response to this unless we are prepared to accept tax schedules that never change. If they do not change, we can use the only non-arbitrary time period there is: a person's lifetime. We could then use annually a system that is actually applied monthly within a year in the Irish PAYE system: cumulative averaging. Under the Irish PAYE system, monthly tax liability depends, not on one's income in that month, but on one's cumulative income since the beginning of the year and, by the end of the year, two people who have the same total annual income will pay the same tax, regardless of the fact that their monthly incomes may fluctuate according to different patterns. In principle, one could do the same on a lifetime basis. However, the system works within a year because the schedule of rates does not change within a year. It could not work over a lifetime because we would not tolerate such lack of change in the rate schedule.

The significance of this inequity depends on the degree of fluctuation in income from tax period to tax period. The Irish system has in fact recognised this by allowing farmers to choose the option of three-year averaging rather than annual income as the basis of assessment. Also, relief for losses under business income taxation can be regarded as a form of multi-year averaging. This kind of ad hoc application of multi-period averaging is probably the best that can be done; although the problem is difficult in principle, in practice it can be recognised only in activities where major year-to-year fluctuations in income exist. It is most obviously serious in regard to capital gains (see Chapter 3).

The definition of the base

The classic prescription for the measure of equal situations is income or wealth since these are obvious measures of a person's command over resources, or a person's ability to spend or save. It is not the only possibility: there is a long tradition that, since the purpose of taxation is to finance public expenditure, equal situations should mean equal benefit from public expenditure. This is an attractive option since it is based on equivalence with the notion that markets are fair because, in markets, people pay what measures the benefit they expect to get from what they purchase. That is, people would pay taxes according to how they value the benefits they received from what the taxes finance. This 'benefit approach', however, presents difficulties. First, it makes impossible any redistribution of welfare through the fiscal system – and most want the fiscal system to redistribute income and/or wealth, at least to some extent. Second, there is the problem of measuring, at the individual level, the value of the benefits received from public expenditure.

For these reasons, the benefit approach is, for general purposes anyway, a non-starter and the ability-to-pay approach remains unchallenged, leaving the question of the proper measure of ability to pay. As already noted, income is the favourite, but that is not the end of the story because the definition of income is not self-evident. The most favoured definition among several generations of tax economists is the so-called 'comprehensive' definition (sometimes called the Haig-Simons definition, after two early proponents). Income is defined in one of two exactly equivalent ways, both based on the fact that income in any period is identically equal to the sum of expenditure and saving (where the latter can be negative) in that period. According to this definition, income in any period is equal to the sum of expenditure during the period and any change in the value of wealth during the period. Alternatively, income is the maximum expenditure that could be incurred without one's wealth being less at the end than at the beginning of the period.

The essence of this definition is that the source of income (spending power) is irrelevant: wages from a secure job are treated the same as dividends from a security that may never again pay a dividend. Above all, capital gains are included in income when they accrue, and not just when they are realised. The central point is that a euro is a euro is a euro: regardless of where it comes from, it has the same effect on spending power. If one accepts this definition, one's concept of horizontal equity must reject the special treatment of particular sources of spending power.

Most tax systems, and the Irish system more than many, are full of special treatments. These will be discussed in detail in Chapter 3, but two Irish examples will serve at this stage to illustrate the point. First, the income of artists, composers and writers is exempt from income tax. That is, a person who has a salary and royalties from music or book sales (perhaps one of my academic colleagues if his works are judged to be of sufficient cultural value), has an income for tax purposes that is less than that of someone who has exactly the same total receipts but in the form of salary alone. Second, owner-occupiers of houses receive an income in the form of imputed rent (they are simultaneously the tenant and the landlord), which obviously influences purchasing power, but this is disregarded for tax purposes. Such discrimination may be regarded by some as proper, but it is misleading to proclaim that it is fair.

Despite the attractiveness of the comprehensive definition, it is not without its difficulties. Take the following example. A person has wealth in the form of bonds valued at €100,000 at the beginning of the period when the rate of interest is 5 per cent. If nothing changes during the period, he has an income of €5,000. But suppose the interest rate rises to 6 per cent, thus causing the value of his bonds to fall to €83,333. So, according to the comprehensive definition, his income is €5,000 less a capital loss (on an accruals basis) of €16,667 – a total income of negative €11,667. Can we accept this? Purists probably would, but it is a conundrum.

Another problem with the comprehensive definition relates to the fact that two people may not gain the same welfare from the same income, comprehensively defined. It can be surmised that, at the margin, a poor person gets more welfare from an extra euro of income than does a rich person (though this presumption can be challenged), but that is a matter for the discussion of vertical equity below. What is at stake here is the possibility that two people with the same income derive different levels of welfare from that income. It is likely that if one of these persons has dependants, he will receive less personal benefit from a given level of income than a person without others to support. That problem can be looked after by giving allowances for dependants. In a sense, that departs from the comprehensive definition of income, but can best be treated as a separate issue. Less tractable is the possibility that two persons with the same income and with the same social commitments may gain different levels of utility from that income. This just has to be accepted as a possibility that cannot be taken account of, because there is no practicable way of giving quantitative expression to the welfare differences.

There is, however, one aspect of this problem that can, in principle anyway, be taken into account. This is the possibility that the utility of a given income depends on the certainty of the source of that income. For example, consider four sources of income: wages from a secure job, labour income from an insecure activity (sport, artistic endeavour or contract work), interest from government securities, and dividends from ordinary shares. The first and third carry little risk, whereas the second and fourth carry a significant risk that the income will not re-occur. Should this distinction matter for the definition of the base of an income tax?

If factor markets worked smoothly, risk would be compensated by higher expected returns. Other things being equal, an insecure job would pay a higher wage and a riskier asset (such as an equity share compared with a government security) would, over the long run, pay the same average return as a less risky asset (the variance of the return would be greater – this is a definition of risk – but high returns in some years would compensate for the lack of dividends or capital gains in other years). If the market did not work like this, the demand for insecure jobs and risky assets would cease to exist. Capital markets certainly converge to this kind of equilibrium more quickly than labour markets and so, unless there is a presumption that the demand for risky assets is somehow non-optimal from the viewpoint of society, there is no need to worry about security of capital income for tax purposes. In the long run, the same applies to labour incomes, but even if it did not it is difficult to see how this could be dealt with in the definition of income.

Equal situations and economic efficiency

When tax systems discriminate among sources of income, the putative reason is usually related to economic efficiency: that is, it is argued that markets will not generate the best available allocation of resources and so certain stimuli (or, conversely, disincentives) need to be provided through the tax system. It will be remembered that horizontal equity does not preclude the making of distinctions among sources of income if those distinctions are non-arbitrary. But suppose a distinction is made on efficiency grounds: what then happens to the concept of horizontal equity? Some would go as far as to say that horizontal equity is an unnecessary concept if tax systems are to be designed according to the canons of economic efficiency. Discrimination among sources of income will be justified as a reaction to the presence of externalities or other forms of market failure; and non-discrimination will be called for in the absence of market failure, not because discrimination would infringe horizontal equity, but because, in such circumstances, non-discrimination would be required by economic efficiency.

To economists anyway, this is a powerful argument. What we look for from the concept of horizontal equity can be entirely catered for under the criterion of economic efficiency. However, as the following reasons show, this may be insufficient. First, discrimination often arises, not from a careful identification of a market failure and a well-judged decision to use the tax system to remedy such a failure, but from the propensity of legislators to respond to pressure groups or what they see as electoral imperatives. Second, perceptions of fairness do far more to influence non-economists' views of tax systems than esoteric notions of economic efficiency, and favours regarded as unfair undermine general compliance. Third, in any given case, uniformity may only trivially infringe economic efficiency because the relevant marginal rates of substitution may be very low and the effect on behaviour (that is on the allocation of resources) may be negligible, whereas the non-uniformity may be perceived as unfair by taxpayers who do not benefit. For these kinds of reason, it is worthwhile maintaining horizontal equity as an independent criterion.

Equal treatment

Discrimination sometimes takes the form of non-uniform definitions of the tax base, which has already been discussed, but it may also take the form of non-uniform schedules of rates. Two examples will serve to illustrate this. First, a VAT that applies different rates to different transactions can be regarded as giving non-equal treatment to those in equal situations. Second, a tax system (such as that in Ireland) that subjects capital gains to a different regime from that applying to other income is, if one accepts the comprehensive definition of income, treating equals unequally. But the distinction between discriminatory definitions of the tax base (the definition of equal situations) and discriminatory tax schedules (unequal treatment) is rather arbitrary and, in the remainder of this book, that distinction will not be employed: what will matter is whether or not *any* discrimination can be justified.

VERTICAL EQUITY

Horizontal equity is concerned with the equal treatment of equals. Vertical equity refers to the relative treatment of those accepted to be in unequal situations, and the issues are most easily reviewed when the tax base is income.

Over the past two centuries, tax economists have tried very hard to develop coherent and practicable answers to these questions. They have made some progress, but not very much. It has been universally agreed that a person's tax bill should increase with his income, but the more interesting question as to precisely how that bill should be related to income is still something to which economics has failed to find a really helpful answer.

This is a question of how progressive the tax schedule should be and, since any answer implies a view as to the extent to which the tax system should redistribute purchasing power among taxpayers, it is also a question of how much redistribution we should look for from that system. Ultimately, this is not an economic issue at all: the extent to which one thinks society should redistribute, say, income, reflects one's view of society and the role that governmental institutions like taxes should play in it. However, over recent years, light has been thrown on these issues by the development of the concept of optimal income taxation, which is central to the current professional debate among tax theorists.

This approach attempts to tackle in tandem the questions of vertical equity and economic efficiency. How this is done can be most easily indicated by reference to the taxation of wage income, as follows. The efficiency criterion requires that the tax should have as small an effect as possible on the supply of labour – that is, on the choice of occupation and on the choice between income and leisure. Clearly, this is satisfied, not by an income tax, but by a lump-sum tax independent of wage income. But such a tax would be severely regressive with respect to income and would therefore infringe any requirement regarding ability to pay. On the other hand, the more egalitarian one's attitude to vertical equity, the higher will be the marginal tax rates one prescribes, but high marginal rates are more likely to infringe the efficiency criterion by influencing decisions about work. This approach is an effort to elucidate the compromise between efficiency and equity considerations.

No matter what the pre-tax distribution of income and no matter how egalitarian one wants to be (as long as one also has an efficiency criterion), the optimal income tax can be approximated by a schedule with only one marginal rate (called a linear income tax). This contradicts the widespread assumption that a strongly redistributive tax requires the familiar stepped structure of marginal rates.[7] The intuition here is that high marginal rates have strong substitution effects on labour supply (or on tax compliance) with two results. First, this distortion seriously infringes the efficiency criterion. This may not worry a very egalitarian government, but the second result should. If high marginal rates cause people to take more leisure – or cause them to avoid or evade tax – the taxable income of those subject to such rates will be lower than if their rates were lower. So, the amount of revenue available to redistribute may actually be lower than if the rates of tax were lower.

Despite all this, nothing in economics tells one *how* redistributive one should be, or how important vertical equity is compared with economic efficiency. Fortunately, the central result of optimal income tax theory tells us that linearity is desirable regardless of this trade-off. It does, however, affect the rate of tax. The more one wants the income tax to generate income to be redistributed to the less well off, the higher that rate has to be, up to a limit where the disincentive effects are so great that any increase in the rate causes revenue to fall. There really is no answer from within economics to such questions, which are a matter of social philosophy.

This discussion has concentrated on income tax because that can be directly tailored to the issue of the different treatment of different individuals. However, the issue of equity also arises with, for example, VAT. We know that the ratio of consumption (the base of VAT) to income falls as income rises and also that the composition of consumption changes as total consumption changes (the rich spend, for example, a lower proportion of total consumption on food and a higher proportion on motoring). This has been used to justify, very obviously in Ireland but to

---

7   Strictly speaking, this kind of tax requires a single rate from zero income upwards. A tax schedule with an exemption and then a single rate will not satisfy this condition since there are really two marginal rates: zero up to the exemption level and then a positive rate. The requirement could be satisfied by having social welfare transfers smoothly related to income up to the exemption level at the same rate as that applying to income above the exemption level.

some extent in most countries, the low taxation of food and the high taxation of cars. That is, differential rates of VAT, combined with selective excises, are justified in an effort to make the system of consumption taxes less regressive with respect to income. The strength of this justification will be considered in Chapter 5.

ADMINISTRATIVE EFFICIENCY

Our review so far has ignored the fact that tax collection is not a costless process. We now address this in the form of a third criterion: administrative efficiency.

The administrative costs of collecting taxes fall into two parts: collection costs borne by the tax authorities and compliance costs borne by the taxpayers. In a sense, these costs are simply wasteful of resources: taxation is just the transfer of purchasing power from the private economy to the state, nothing being produced. It is appropriate, therefore, that we should want, other things being equal, a system that keeps these costs to a minimum.

There being no general principles to which we can appeal, the question of administrative efficiency is best addressed by means of examples. Take first the personal income tax. The Irish income tax structure, which was inherited from the British, still bears the marks of a system that treated different sources of income differently – what is called a schedular system. Ireland still has its income tax divided into schedules, which refer to income from different sources. The essential feature of a schedular system is that income from different sources is not aggregated, each schedule applying what is essentially a separate tax. Ireland, of course, does aggregate income from different sources for most (but not all) purposes and the relics of the old schedular system are of less substantive importance than they may appear. However, many less-developed tax systems, notably in Africa and Asia, do employ a truly schedular system – the reason being that it is much simpler, and therefore cheaper, to apply than a global system that aggregates income from all sources. So, the global system better meets both efficiency and equity criteria (it is essential for a comprehensive income tax), but imposes greater administrative costs than a schedular system because someone (in fact a combination of the taxpayer and tax collector) has to perform the aggregation.

Ireland does retain aspects of a true schedular system where there is final withholding of tax at source. In some cases involving the payment of interest, the payer (bank, building society etc.) withholds tax at a flat rate and there is no more liability with respect to that income: there is *final* withholding. Such interest income is not aggregated with, say, wages in the hands of the recipient for income tax purposes. Such a system of final withholding certainly reduces administrative costs by avoiding the need for aggregation, but may infringe both efficiency and equity criteria by discriminating according to the source of income.

One example of withholding, the PAYE system as applied to employment income, is interesting for a different reason. It is not final withholding because if an employee has another source of income not subject to final withholding, the two sources are aggregated for the purposes of the annual assessment. The PAYE system is in itself, therefore, consistent with the efficiency and equity criteria. It is interesting, not because it reduces total administrative costs (though it almost certainly does), but because it changes the distribution of those costs. If there were no PAYE system, each employee would have to file an annual return and his employer would be involved only if required to provide evidence in support of such a return or in the event of a taxpayer audit by the tax authorities. Almost all the compliance costs would fall on the employee. Under PAYE, an employee with no income other than wages from one employer has no obligation to file a return: indeed, he will normally have no dealings at all with the tax authorities, except to claim allowances or in the comparatively rare cases where the PAYE system has extracted too much or too little tax from him. The tax authorities have to send the employer a statement for each employee showing allowed deductions and the rate at which tax is to be withheld. Periodically, the employer has to account for, and pay over, the tax withheld. Furthermore, the peculiarly Irish and British PAYE systems (involving cumulative application within a year) require documentation to be issued by the employer when an employee leaves. The result of all this is the imposition of significant costs on the employer, whereas the costs borne by the employee are almost zero and those borne by the tax authorities are reduced, there being fewer employers than employees and so fewer collection points. Of course, this is only the formal incidence of the costs. In the face of these new costs, employers must either reduce their wage bill or suffer a decline in profits. If they do the former, the incidence is at least partly shifted back to the employees.

Another feature that changes the distribution of administrative costs is self-assessment, which is used in Ireland for VAT and the taxation of business income. This shifts the costs to the taxpayer, leaving the tax authorities with little more than the costs of audit and taxpayer information.

Sometimes administrative costs can be so great that they influence the structure of the tax system. Thus, capital gains are taxed as they are realised, rather than as they accrue which is what the comprehensive definition of income would require. This is because an accrual basis would involve the annual valuation of all assets, which would be very expensive to undertake, especially for assets where there is not a continuously functioning, reasonably competitive market. This difficulty in valuing assets at regular intervals explains why relatively few countries have a general wealth tax. Ireland had one for three years in the mid-1970s, but the high administrative cost was one of the reasons for its abolition.

The simpler the structure of a tax, the lower its administrative costs. This is of particular pertinence to Ireland, where basic taxes (income tax and VAT) are very complex and non-uniform. In its essence, VAT is quite cheap to administer. It is self-assessed, which keeps collection costs low, but the compliant taxpayer requires only the fairly rudimentary record-keeping that any prudent trader would want for his own purposes. But the Irish VAT zero-rates major items of domestic consumption, exempts a wide range of transactions, and has several positive rates. This complexity increases the compliance costs of traders, who have to split their sales and purchases into several categories according to whether or not they are zero-rated, whether or not they are exempt and which positive rate applies. Collection costs increase as the tax authorities strive to police these divisions. The fact that the authorities have limited resources means that this policing will not be totally effective and so the incentive to evade is increased.

Income tax is much worse in this respect. Merely to illustrate, consider the fact that the income of artists, composers and authors is exempt as long as the works in question have been given a certificate of cultural value by the relevant ministry. That ministry incurs costs in this certification process and the tax authorities have to be satisfied that the income for which exemption is claimed is solely derived from certified works. Similar 'policing' costs are incurred in relation to concessions such as the business expansion scheme, the special reliefs available to film production and geographically discriminating favours to certain types of investment in real property.

The huge array of discriminatory provisions in the Irish income tax places extra costs on the taxpayer wishing to be compliant (and on the authorities in checking that compliance) and creates a whole industry of tax consultants who sell compliance services and advice on tax minimisation schemes. It also opens the door to illegal evasion (one man's incentive is another man's loophole). For example, large numbers of bank accounts were fraudulently claimed to be owned by non-residents so as to avoid the withholding tax on interest (DIRT). It was the discriminatory exemption of non-resident accounts that created the opportunity for evasion.

BALANCING THE CRITERIA

If the criteria reviewed above were not in conflict with each other, tax policy would be easy. However, usually a tax provision will accord with one criterion but conflict with another and so even policymakers who wish to apply those criteria have to find some method of 'trade-off' among them.[8] We have noted one case where this process has been investigated analytically – optimal income taxation as a balance between efficiency and vertical equity – but the more general problem has been little investigated and throws up almost intractable difficulties.

Economics can assist the understanding of these difficulties, but has little to contribute to their solution. Perhaps the most difficult conflict arises between economic efficiency and horizontal equity. A review of the literature suggests that many tax economists have in recent years changed their (implicit) trade-off between these criteria, as is evidenced by the declining prominence given to the comprehensive definition of income, which is the dominant approach to the application of horizontal equity.

---

8   As will often be apparent in subsequent pages, much of the Irish tax system conflicts with all of these criteria, the presumed reason being that another criterion (which may loosely be called political) is dominant. Here, we are dealing only with the reviewed criteria.

Let us illustrate this by reference to the question of whether labour and capital income should be taxed similarly.

Given the fact that horizontal equity would seem to demand equality of treatment of all factor incomes, the trade-off should be determined by the scale of the welfare loss that equal treatment could generate: the larger it is, the stronger the case for breaching the equity criterion. Since the welfare loss resulting from taxation depends upon the extent to which the tax distorts behaviour – that is, the elasticities of demand for, and supply of, the object of the tax – the case for taxing capital more lightly rests upon the assertion that these elasticities are larger in the case of capital than in the case of labour. With globalisation and the fact that capital is internationally more mobile than labour (because migration costs are lower), the elasticity of supply of capital in a given country is even higher than it was. Thus, the case on efficiency grounds for taxing capital more lightly than labour is even stronger than it was, and hence the increased attention given to this in the trade-off with horizontal equity (and, indeed, vertical equity, since recipients of capital income tend to be richer than those relying on their wages).

This argument establishes that there is a case for differential taxation of capital income and that this case is stronger than it was, but it tells us nothing about how to balance this against the loss of horizontal equity between workers and *rentiers*. At the core of the difficulty is the fact that we can, in principle and sometimes in practice, measure the welfare gain from improved economic efficiency, get some quantified clue as to the administrative costs of differential taxation and measure (again in principle and often in practice) the impact of such taxation on the distribution of net incomes, which is relevant to vertical equity; on the other hand, there is no way of putting a number on the loss of horizontal equity. We can recognise the magnitude of the differential, but this tells us nothing about whether this differential constitutes a loss of horizontal equity large enough to offset any net gains relating to the other criteria.

In essence, the importance one attaches to horizontal equity depends upon two factors. First, the extent to which one accepts that, say, efficiency considerations constitute relevant differences, in the sense that good laws are supposed to discriminate among persons only according to relevant differences. But this is just another way of stating the problem of weighing a loss of horizontal equity against gains under other criteria. Second, there is an issue rarely alluded to in the economic literature: horizontal equity is the criterion of most concern to taxpayers in that they are likely to be conscious of a case where they see themselves as treated more harshly than others. Acceptance that taxes are reasonably fair is a critical factor in inducing widespread compliance with tax laws. Most of us would feel less compunction in evading tax if we believed that others are favoured by the tax system: the moral incentive to evade is increased if the system is seen as unfair. If we have little opportunity to evade (because, for instance, all of our income comes from wages subject to PAYE), our disenchantment may take a more political form – as it did in Ireland in the late 1970s.

For this kind of reason, I would probably give more importance to horizontal equity than would be typical nowadays among my professional colleagues. However, that is a personal preference. As yet we have no technical means of assisting policymakers in balancing this most difficult criterion against the other criteria reviewed here.

3

The Taxation of Income and Capital Gains

The structure of income tax is of dominant importance in any consideration of tax reform. First, it accounts for a large proportion of total revenue: income taxes in the broad sense represent almost 60 per cent of total taxes. Second, since income tax directly distinguishes among individuals, its equity is a central concern, both vertically and horizontally. Third, there is a non-trivial degree of substitutability among different sources of income, between consumption and saving and between income and leisure (or unpaid work) and so distortions – that is, infringements of the criterion of economic efficiency – must be a worry. The other side of this coin is that discriminatory income taxes are favourite instruments for governments who wish to use the tax system to encourage or reward behaviour of which they approve. If the comprehensive definition of income is, even approximately, accepted as appropriate, discrimination among the various sources of income is not obviously justifiable on either equity or efficiency grounds, and such discrimination will provide a leitmotiv of this chapter.

Irish income taxes come in four guises: the income tax proper, which applies to individual persons (or certain groups, such as spouses and children, who may be treated collectively under the income tax) and non-incorporated businesses; the corporation tax, which applies to the profits of companies; the capital gains tax, which applies to gains arising on the trade or disposal of assets, and is here regarded as an income tax; and social welfare contributions, the base of which is labour income.

Before proceeding, a caveat needs to be entered. Irish income taxes are very complex and no attempt is made here to capture all the details. Instead, the focus will be on rather broad structural issues, using detailed provisions essentially as illustrations of the more general points at issue.

INCOME TAX

In general, income taxes can be divided into two types: schedular and global. Under the former, income is divided according to the nature of the source (wages, rent, interest etc.) and receipts from each source are taxed separately, sometimes with different rate structures and always having the distinctive feature that the income from different sources is not aggregated for tax purposes. Under a global system, income from all sources is aggregated and then subjected to a universal rate structure.

Ireland's income tax is, in broad terms, global, but it has certain schedular features which will be dealt with as we proceed. The most obvious schedular feature concerns nomenclature in that the different sources of income are labelled by reference to schedules. Schedule C refers to interest on securities issued by public bodies. Schedule D refers to rents, interest not chargeable under Schedule C and non-corporate profits. Schedule E refers to wages, salaries[1] and other remuneration from employment, and certain social welfare benefits. Schedule F refers to dividends.[2] Schedules A and B covered income from the occupation and ownership of land, but they were abolished in 1969 and, since 1974, income formerly covered by Schedule B is included under Schedule D. Certain provisions for deductions vary between schedules (and between cases within a schedule), but the important point is that these schedules are no more than convenient labels. Although certain types of income may be treated differently from others, this discrimination could operate without the schedular nomenclature. The Irish income tax is, in broad terms, global, in that the total tax liability of a person receiving income

---

1   The archaic distinction between wage and salary will not be used here: all cash remuneration from employment will be simply called wages.
2   There is a portmanteau provision (Case IV of Schedule D) that captures income not falling under any other schedule and not explicitly exempt.

under more than one schedule is, by and large, determined by the aggregation of all income.[3]

The basic structure

In 2001, two fundamental changes were made to the basis of the income tax: certain allowances or deductions were converted to tax credits, and the treatment of married couples was changed.

An allowance reduces taxable income and so the tax saved by an allowance is equal to the value of the allowance multiplied by the relevant marginal tax rate. A tax credit, on the other hand, constitutes a direct reduction in tax liability. What may be called 'gross' liability is calculated as if there were no allowance or credit and then the 'net' liability is determined by deducting the value of the credit. Essentially, all of what were previously known as personal allowances – that is, the basic personal allowance for single or married persons, the widowed person's allowance, the widowed parent's allowance, the one-parent family allowance, the blind person's allowance, the age allowance, and the allowances for incapacitated children and dependent relatives – have been converted to credits. In addition, the tax-free PAYE allowance against Schedule E income, the home carer allowance and the allowance for trade union subscriptions were converted to credits.

Persons with especially low incomes may opt for a special exemption rather than a personal credit. Since the low-income exemption depends upon the number of children, this option is effectively relevant only to persons with several children because for those with few children the personal credit is more valuable than the exemption.

The purpose of the conversion of allowances to credits is to make the system more progressive. Thus, a standard allowance is worth more in terms of tax saved if the marginal rate is greater (in other words, the higher the income), whereas a standard credit is worth the same regardless of income. In effect, the adoption of credits allows one to give more prominence to vertical equity without the potential efficiency cost of increasing marginal rates.

---

3   The qualification refers primarily to the fact that some income is subject to final withholding at the standard tax rate and so that income is not aggregated with other income.

Two issues need mention. First, Irish credits are not refundable: that is, if the 'gross' liability is less than the credit, the balance is merely lost by the taxpayer. There is no cash refund and the balance of the credit may not be carried forward for use in a subsequent tax year. While attractive in terms of administrative simplicity (not generally a consideration in the Irish income tax), the non-refundability aspect certainly makes the credits less effective in terms of progressivity (as it is those at the lowest end of the income scale who lose from the absence of refunds or carry-forward provisions). The lack of refunds perpetuates one of the difficulties with the old scheme of personal allowances: an increase in the allowance gave no benefit to a person whose gross income was so low as to fall short of the existing allowance.

The second issue concerns the type of allowance or deduction that should be replaced by a credit. In principle, if the argument for credits holds water at all, it does so for all deductions or allowances. However, credits can get complicated if applied to deductible expenditures because it is not possible to have a standard credit. A compromise, which is applied to certain of the remaining allowances, is to grant an allowance only at the lowest marginal rate (the standard rate) rather than at the actual marginal rate for any given taxpayer.

The tax credits which apply to most taxpayers are shown in Table 3.1.

Table 3.1: Selected tax credits (€ per year), 2003

	Tax credit
Single	1,520
Married	3,040
PAYE	800

Tax credits and tax rates combine in the following way. The first slice of income is taxed at 20 per cent and the remainder at 42 per cent. This determines the 'gross' liability, from which any credit is deducted to give the 'net' liability. The interesting issues concern the first slice or the standard rate bracket. These brackets are set out in Table 3.2.

Table 3.2: Standard rate brackets (€ per year), 2003

	Taxable income*
Single/widowed	1–28,000
Married one income	1–37,000
Married two incomes	1–56,000**
Single parent	1–32,000

* Income after allowances but before credit
** Transferable between spouses up to €37,000 for any one spouse

The most significant point here concerns the treatment of married couples. From 1980 to 2001[4], the Irish income tax applied what was essentially an income-splitting system to spouses who elected to be taxed jointly. Income was aggregated between spouses and the aggregate then attracted a personal allowance twice that applicable to single persons (or married persons electing to be taxed separately) and rate brackets double those applying to single persons (or, again, married persons taxed separately). The effect was to impose a joint tax liability equal to that payable in total if the couple were taxed separately and had equal incomes. It made no difference whether each or only one spouse had an income.

The system implemented in 2001 was intended as the first step towards a completely individualistic definition of the tax unit – that is, a system which treats spouses as if they were single persons. This step involved distinguishing among married couples according to whether they have one or two incomes. However, this strategy of individualisation occasioned what was probably the most vigorous public outcry on a tax matter for twenty years or so and, at the time of writing, only the first step has been taken. The debate essentially involved the considerations reviewed in Chapter 2 concerning the tax unit. The main issue is whether there is any justification for distinguishing among married couples according to whether they have one or two incomes. There is certainly no justification in horizontal equity. That principle can be appealed to to support income-

---

4   Strictly, until 5 April 2001. Until 2001, the income tax year always ended on 5 April. From 2002, the tax year has been the calendar year, with an intervening 'short year' of 6 April to 31 December 2001.

splitting or individualisation, but not the current intermediate position. Where it may be justified is in relation to economic efficiency. Aggregation and income-splitting often impose a high marginal rate on a spouse who is contemplating entering the formal labour force. Under the present system, a couple, where a previously 'non-earning' spouse becomes an earner, has its standard rate bracket extended from €37,000 to €56,000: that is, the newly earning spouse faces a rate of only 20 per cent on the first €19,000 of his earnings.

A flavour of the degree of progressivity can be gained from the sample of gross incomes in Table 3.3, which shows effective tax rates (tax as a percentage of gross income) for taxpayers with no allowances (that is, where only the personal tax credit, the PAYE credit and the normal rate brackets are relevant). For this illustration, all income is assumed to be taxable under Schedule E and married couples elect for joint taxation.

Table 3.3: Selected effective rates of income tax (% of gross income), 2003

Gross income	Single	Married 1*	Married 2**
10,000	0	0	0
15,000	4.5	0	0
20,000	8.4	0.8	0
25,000	10.7	4.6	1.4
30,000	13.7	7.2	4.5
40,000	20.8	12.1	8.4
60,000	27.9	22.0	13.7
100,000	33.5	30.0	25.0
150,000	36.3	34.0	30.7

* a married couple with one income
** a married couple with two incomes

Table 3.4 shows the tax saving achieved by married couples with a given total income if both spouses are earning.

Table 3.4: Tax saving with two earners (€), 2003

Gross income	Saving
10,000	0
15,000	0
20,000	160
25,000	800
30,000	800
40,000	1,460
60,000	4,980
100,000	4,980
150,000	4,980

Tables 3.3 and 3.4 show very clearly the conflict between equity and efficiency occasioned by the more favourable treatment of married couples where both spouses earn. Any efficiency gain produced by the encouragement to a previously non-earning spouse to enter the labour force has to be balanced by the loss of vertical (and, some would argue, horizontal) equity. Perhaps the biggest defect of the current system is that the increase in the standard rate bracket given to two-earner couples is not restricted to couples where both are in the labour force (although, of course, both would have to be in the labour force to qualify for two PAYE credits). Thus, if the wife is an employee but the husband has no formal income, there is a large incentive to ensure that any non-wage income (such as rents or interest on joint savings) is at least partially put in the name of the husband alone. He then becomes an earner for these purposes and so the two-earner standard bracket applies. 'Earner' simply means 'has an income', and the income does not have to be a wage. This kind of tax planning has no efficiency gain (it is a distortion that could create an efficiency loss), but the reduction in equity is still there. If the only efficiency gain claimed for this device is the lower marginal rate faced by a spouse contemplating waged work, then it would be more sensible to restrict the concept of two earners to two wage-earners.

But the whole approach is fundamentally confused. There is no obvious reason why a spouse should gain a tax advantage by entering the labour force rather than engaging in domestic work, since there is no necessary advantage to society as a whole if he works outside rather than inside the home. GDP rises, but that is the result of the fact that GDP includes waged but not unwaged work. The increase in GDP does not necessarily imply any increase in the welfare of society.

Further confusion is introduced by the availability of an additional credit (the home carer's credit) if the 'non-working' spouse stays at home to look after children. This is an attempt to partially rectify the bias in favour of those spouses who work outside the home, but the method is incoherent. It can be argued that children share in their parents' income and so should be treated in qualitatively the same way as a non-earning spouse. The current carer's credit is no more than an ad hoc reaction to the outcry occasioned by the granting of more favourable treatment to couples comprising two earners rather than one.

A final issue in the basic structure concerns the thresholds and widths of the brackets. Allowances, credits and brackets are defined in nominal terms and if they are not adjusted in the face of inflation, there is a non-legislated increase in real effective tax rates – a phenomenon known as bracket-creep – because the real value of these parameters declines. This has not been a problem recently in Ireland. Although the real value of personal allowances fell in the early 1990s, in 2003 it was more than twice what it had been ten years earlier. This reflects the policy response to two factors: the increase in average real incomes over the previous decade and the desire to move the threshold for tax higher up the income distribution, thus removing former taxpayers from the net. Thus, the equivalent of the single personal allowance is now around 30 per cent of the average industrial wage, whereas, ten years previously, it was about 15 per cent.

Non-business allowances and deductions

We here review the deductions that are available with respect to certain *uses* of income. Deductions for business expenses are dealt with later, as is discriminatory treatment of certain sources of income. The major uses of income that attract allowances are medical expenses; medical insurance premiums; residential rental payments; fees at third-level educational institutions and for certain types of training; pension contributions; interest on residential mortgages and, in some cases, loans taken out to finance unquoted companies; and certain donations. There is also a credit with respect to payments to local authorities for refuse disposal ('bin charges'). The fact that this particular tax attracts relief from income tax, whereas other taxes which are akin to user charges do not, suggests that it was a political response to the unpopularity of the charges.

Two points are fundamental to a consideration of deductions: the comprehensive definition of income would grant deductibility only to expenditure necessarily and solely arising in the course of gaining taxable income; and there are arguments as to whether income saved should be exempt from tax.

Housing

The issues here are whether or not *any* housing expenses should be deductible and whether owner-occupiers should be treated differently from tenants. Mortgage interest is deductible, with respect to the main residence, up to a maximum of €3,175 for a single person on a mortgage taken out since 1998 (and €2,540 for an earlier mortgage), these limits being doubled for a married couple. When this deduction was first introduced, it could be justified under the comprehensive definition of income because the imputed rental income of owner-occupiers was taxed under Schedule A.[5] Since the abolition of that schedule in 1969, however, this allowance is granted despite the fact that the expenditure in question is not incurred for the purposes of earning taxed income. It is, therefore, a straight subsidy to a particular use of income.

The first thing to note is that there is not parity between owner-occupiers and tenants. A tax credit is available to tenants of €254 for a single person and double that for a married or widowed person if the claimant is under 55 years of age, with both being doubled again if the claimant is over 55 years old. Why older tenants are favoured is a mystery. The tenant pays rent to the landlord, who then has to pay tax on his rental income. On the other hand, an owner-occupier (someone who is simultaneously tenant and landlord) is favoured because, although mortgage interest (equivalent to part of the 'rent') is partially deductible, the (imputed) income is not taxable.

We thus have multiple distortions. If you have a sum to invest, there is a tax advantage in using it to buy a house in which you will live, because

---

5   Imputed income is the rent that an owner-occupier, as a tenant, notionally pays to himself as a landlord.

the benefit (housing services) will not be taxed. Whereas, if you invest it in another type of asset (including a house which you rent out), the benefit (cash income) will usually be taxed. If your income rises and you decide you can afford to service a loan financing a purchase, there is a tax advantage in buying a bigger house in which you will live rather than, say, a new car or a series of nice holidays, since the interest on the larger mortgage will be tax-deductible whereas the interest on loans for other purchases will usually not be.[6] If you need accommodation, the rental tax credit will be €254 if you are single and €508 if you are married, whereas the tax saved by the maximum mortgage interest deduction (which is granted at the 20 per cent rate) will be €635 and €1,270 respectively.

How can this privileged treatment of a particular type of consumption be justified? Is there something special about owner-occupation? Of course housing is a necessity, but food is even more so and there is no income tax favour for eating. In any case, it is the particular favour to owner-occupation that is at stake here. The usual argument for this favour is that society at large benefits if owner-occupation is extensive. It provides an especially valuable form of personal security that makes society more stable. Despite its repetition, this argument is never supported empirically. The prevalence of owner-occupation varies considerably among countries with the same level of economic, political and social development, but there is no evidence that stability (whatever that is) is affected by the extent to which occupiers own their housing. Also, the assertion that people are happier if they own their own housing is not relevant: if that were the case, tax favours would be unnecessary since voluntary choice would load the dice in favour of owner-occupation.

The fact of the matter is that this is an example of electoral influence on tax policy – and in this case there are a lot of votes at stake. It also reflects the political difficulty of withdrawing a favour once given. When the imputed income of owner-occupiers was taxed under Schedule A, the deductibility of mortgage interest made sense. When that taxation was abolished, the change was extremely popular among the home-owning classes and the policymakers did not want to put the kudos they earned at risk by eliminating mortgage relief. However, that would have been the time to do it: balancing an unpopular change against a popular change. If

---

6   An exception to this generalisation would be a loan to purchase certain shares.

that relief were to be abolished now, another popular balancing change would have to be found.

Perhaps the solution would be to re-introduce the taxation of imputed income but to allow full deductibility, at the appropriate marginal rate, of mortgage interest. We would then have something coherent. A corollary would be that the rental credit would be abolished.[7] The real difficulty with the old Schedule A was not its existence, but the way it worked. The valuation was based on the system in place for local property taxes (rates, abolished in 1978 with respect to residences) and this was known to be riddled with inequities. Modern valuation procedures, used widely in other countries for property taxes, would need to be adopted and applied in a way that is seen to be fair. Nor should this idea be rejected on the grounds that it involves the taxation of non-cash income. We already do this with regard to benefits in kind, including housing provided by an employer to an employee.

Admittedly, there is a degree of arbitrariness in taxing the imputed income from residential owner-occupation and not that from the ownership and use of other non-financial assets (cars, yachts, pictures and so on), but it can be justified. The distortion to the housing market produced by our failure to tax the imputed income from owner-occupation is far greater than that produced in other asset markets by a similar failure. Furthermore, it is much easier to construct an effective valuation procedure for residences than for other assets. Finally, the value of houses is greater than the value of other assets and so the net revenue implications are greater.

In changing the basis of taxation of income (including imputed income) from capital, the greatest problem is that the existing effective tax rates have, at least to some extent, been capitalised in the price of the relevant assets. Tax favours to home owners increase the price of housing because purchasers can afford to pay more for their housing than they would if the favours did not exist. This was seen dramatically in the late 1970s when there was a surge in house prices following the abolition of domestic rates (property taxes). The implication is that owner-occupiers

---

7   Rental credit has the administrative virtue that the claiming tenant is obliged to identify the landlord, which helps in the taxation of rental income. It is impossible to know whether the revenue lost from the credit is exceeded by the extra revenue gained by the improved taxation of rents.

have actually bought the tax favour and so its abolition would generate windfall losses for those owning homes at the time of the abolition.

Opinion is divided as to the proper policy response to this dilemma. At one extreme are those who would take this as an argument for retaining the tax favour, but that implies that we should lock ourselves into the existing provisions, no matter how defective we think they are. At the other extreme are those who would ignore the possibility of windfall losses. There is something to be said for this in the case of housing because most sales are by people who intend to buy another house. The windfall loss on the sale of the existing house would then be offset by the fact that the new house will be cheaper than it would be under the existing tax regime. An intermediate position would be to phase in the abolition of the favour over a number of years so that the change in house prices is gradual. This position was actually taken in Ireland in reducing the extent to which mortgage interest attracts an allowance. The deductibility of mortgage interest, although it is still in existence, is much less generous that it was previously.

Medical expenses

Medical insurance premiums are deductible at the standard rate, there being a kind of reverse withholding with the insurer reducing the premium by 20 per cent and receiving the difference from the Revenue Commissioners. Medical expenses exceeding €125 that are not reimbursed by an insurer are deductible at the relevant marginal rate.

In general, such deductions are not compatible with the comprehensive definition of income since they are not incurred in earning a taxable income. They are a form of voluntary consumption. No-one is obliged to take out medical insurance, and a high proportion of medical expenses are on elective diagnosis and treatment. A case could perhaps be made in equity for redistribution from the well to the sick, but the current practice meets none of the criteria we would demand of such a scheme. Medical expenses are deductible at the relevant marginal rate and so this relief makes the system less progressive.

Any rationale for these reliefs comes from the fact that Ireland does not have a universal health service that is free at the point of delivery. Such a service is, in general, available only to those on lower incomes. Tax deductions can therefore be interpreted as a partial subsidisation of those whose income is too great to enable them to participate in the public health service. This principle makes some sense, but the form of the relief, especially for medical expenses, does not. Suppose we divide the population into low, middle and high incomes, where the last two have marginal tax rates of 20 and 42 per cent respectively. The first has all of its expenses paid from the public purse; the second has 20 per cent of them paid in that way, and the last has 42 per cent paid. This pattern is incoherent. It could be improved by allowing medical expenses only at the standard rate.

Pension contributions

This is a special case of the tax treatment of saving, which is dealt with later in this chapter.

PAYE credit

A long-standing issue is whether or not the comprehensive definition is defective in treating a euro of labour income as equivalent to a euro of income from capital. It has been argued that the former is less secure in that it is vulnerable to unemployment or sickness whereas the latter is not. Therefore, the two euros do not, according to this argument, represent the same ability to pay and so labour income should be treated more favourably. This constitutes the main rationale for the PAYE credit, but the argument is weak in that the tax system takes no account of the insecurity of other kinds of income.[8] Large elements of capital income (notably dividends) are even less secure than wages, but special treatment is not available in such cases. Once again, the political history of this credit is more revealing than principles. Public dissatisfaction with the tax system was expressed in an assertion that the 'PAYE sector' bore an unfairly large part of the burden: the credit (previously an allowance) was introduced as a reaction. Similarly, the totally groundless credit for trade union subscriptions has to be seen as an element in the process of national pay bargaining.

Third-level education and training courses

The allowance (at the standard rate, with a maximum) for fees paid for third-level courses and for training courses in information technology and

---

8   The PAYE credit may also be regarded as compensation for the fact that wages are taxed on a current-year basis, whereas business income is taxed on a prior-year basis.

foreign languages is also difficult to justify. Participation in higher education is positively related to (parental) income and so the benefit from this allowance accrues in an anti-egalitarian manner. This infringement of vertical equity could be justified only if there is an efficiency argument for the tax favour. The argument usually put forward is that there is an external economy associated with higher education and certain types of training – that is, society gains a benefit and so this expenditure would be undertaken at a sub-optimal level in the absence of subsidisation. But this argument is weak: a great deal of research has been undertaken around the world and, at the time of writing, no evidence has been produced that participation in higher education generates any significant positive externality. The whole of the benefit accrues to the participant and there is no evidence of market failure. The same applies to the training courses which attract a tax allowance. The market rewards those who take these courses, and so it is difficult to find a reason for subsidising them to spend their time in this way.

Donations

The issues arising over the deductibility of donations to charities and similar approved bodies are rather different. Much tax-financed public expenditure is on things which, a century ago, were provided by charities alone. Today, many bodies, the donations to which attract tax relief, receive direct subsidies from government. The boundary between public (or publicly assisted) and private charitable provision is therefore fluid and tax deductibility can be regarded as a substitute for public expenditure.[9] In some respects, tax allowances are superior. Suppose a charity receives €1,000 from a donation. If the taxpayer has a marginal rate of 42 per cent, the total €1,000 has come in two parts: €580 from the taxpayer and €420 from the exchequer. So, under this scenario, only €420 has to come from involuntary tax payments, which are certain to have economically distortionary effects, and €580 comes from a voluntary donation, which has no such implications for economic efficiency. The alternative is a tax-financed grant of €1,000, with much greater efficiency effects.

The weakness in this argument is the same as that applying to all allowances or credits designed to reward approved behaviour. The

---

9   Indeed, tax allowances in general are often called tax expenditures.

donation may have been made anyway, in which case the efficiency loss produced by the need to replace the revenue surrendered through the allowance is pure waste. We cannot know what would have happened in the absence of the allowance. It is possible that a smaller donation would have been given anyway, but it is implausible to suggest that the whole of the donation is a response to the incentive given through the allowance.

Exempt income

Certain income is totally or partially exempt from tax. This is in clear breach of the comprehensive definition and so very good reasons would have to be advanced if these exemptions are to be justified. Exemptions and other concessions on business income are dealt with later.

Elderly persons

Persons over 64 years of age are entitled to an income of €13,000 free of tax if single or widowed and €26,000 if married (only one spouse needs to be over 64). Those with incomes above these levels attract additional tax credits of €205 for single/widowed and €410 for married, which, along with the standard personal credits, effectively make the first €8,625 (or €17,250 for couples) free of tax. Since the personal credits for younger persons make only the first €7,600 (or €15,200 for couples) effectively free of tax, this is a significant concession to the elderly.

Why should two persons with the same income and the same relevant other characteristics be treated differently simply because they have different ages? Although age is not a discretionary feature of a person, there could still be distortions because of the incentive offered to a younger person to put some of his own income into the hands of an elderly relative. More importantly, the discrimination is inconsistent with horizontal equity. An aged person with a given income has either the same or a greater ability to pay taxes than a younger person with the same income. He has, usually, no expenses relating to children (which in general attract no allowances or credits). He may have higher medical expenses, but these are deductible anyway. He even receives free public transport. Apart from a vague notion that we should be nice to older people, this concession has no coherent rationale.

Artists and sportspeople

Artists, authors and composers, who are fully resident in Ireland and who receive royalties or similar income from original and creative work of cultural or artistic merit, are completely exempt from tax on that income. The judgement regarding cultural or artistic merit is made by the tax authorities according to ministerial guidelines. This concession is, as far as I know, unique in the world and it has no merit whatsoever. The income in question may be uncertain or fluctuating, but no more so than receipts from other activities that receive no special privileges.

The public justification relies on the assertion that it is a social benefit if such persons are attracted to live in Ireland, but this assertion is opaque in the extreme. I gain benefit from listening to the compositions or reading the books in question, but it makes no difference to that enjoyment whether or not the composers or authors live here (in fact, my tastes tend to run to the works of those who are dead). How is the cultural life of the nation enhanced by the local residence of writers of pop songs or airport novels that have been given the certificate of cultural approval? The whole thing was the brainchild of a Minister for Finance in the 1970s who fancied himself as a patron of the arts and no subsequent politician has had the nerve to repeal it.

In 2002, a Minister for Finance, whose personal tastes were of a more sporting nature, sponsored a similar scheme for professional exponents of athletics, badminton, boxing, cycling, football, golf, horse racing (jockeys), motor racing (drivers), rugby, squash, swimming and tennis (but not darts or snooker, or even cricket!). When a sportsperson retires and resides in Ireland, he can claim relief in the form of a deduction equal to 40 per cent of income (net of expenses) earned in the previous ten years, the relief taking the form of repayment of tax. It could be argued that this provision is an attempt to recognise the fluctuating nature of sporting income; however, if that is the problem, it should be dealt with by the kind of averaging available to farmers.

No doubt chefs eagerly await the installation of a gastronome as minister!

Social welfare benefits

Many social welfare benefits are taxable under Schedule E, but some (essentially those of a short-term nature) are not. Exempt from tax are:

unemployment assistance (paid to the unemployed who do not qualify for unemployment benefit, which is taxable), maternity benefit, children's allowance (paid with respect to all children regardless of the income or other characteristics of the parents), death grant, disability allowance and family income supplement (payable to those with no income whose characteristics deny them other benefits such as unemployment assistance).

In many cases (very obviously as regards unemployment assistance and family income supplement), the exemption is of little significance because, as a result of the personal tax credit, the recipient would pay no tax even if the receipt had been in principle taxable. Maternity and death benefits can be ignored because they are very short term. The biggest issue concerns children's allowances and recently there has been some public debate over the tax-free status of these grants.

The children's allowance under the social welfare system can be thought of as a substitute for tax allowances or credits for children, which used to exist but are no longer.[10] It is superior to a tax allowance because the effective value is unrelated to the marginal rate, but not obviously superior to a tax credit. (It could be regarded as equivalent to a *refundable* tax credit – other credits are not refundable – but the attitude taken here is that this allowance is better regarded as a form of income.) A fundamental question concerns whether this payment is justified at all, but this raises the same issues as the choice of tax unit, which were dealt with in Chapter 2, and, in any case, it is a matter of social welfare rather than tax policy. The tax policy question concerns the tax exemption.

The problem is that the exemption reduces the progressivity of the system: if the payments were taxable, the net benefit would decline with the marginal rate. The argument usually put forward for the exemption is that, as long as the children live with the mother, the allowance is paid to the mother and is a publicly operated form of inter-spousal transfer designed to cope with the, allegedly prevalent, problem that fathers make insufficient provision for the upkeep of their offspring. To the author this argument sounds condescending and (as a father) personally insulting and goes no distance at all in justifying tax-exempt payments to families who can well afford the consequences of their own choices.

---

10 Although there is a home carer's credit when one spouse looks after his children on a full-time basis.

Benefits in kind

Benefits in kind are non-cash perquisites provided directly or indirectly by an employer to an employee (or by a company to a director). In general, they should be valued and taxed as if they were wages in monetary form – otherwise there would be an inequity between someone who receives such benefit and someone who receives equal value in money, and there would be a distortionary incentive to remunerate employees by means of non-cash benefits.

How should the value of the benefit be assessed? One possible answer is to take the amount the employee would be prepared to pay for the services in question. This is attractive in that it derives from the very basis of the normative justification for market transactions – that is, someone making a purchase values that purchase by putting his money where his mouth is. The problem is in applying this notion. Take the case of an airline employee who gets a free return ticket to Australia as a bonus. The market price of this ticket is €1,500. However, the employee may well be prepared to forego the trip if he had to pay for it himself – that is, he may value it at much less than €1,500. There is no way of knowing how much he valued a free ticket. The second possibility is the cost to the employer. This may be practicable in some cases, but not in all. Again, take an airline employee who gets a free seat on that airline. The cost to his employer would be zero if the seat would otherwise be vacant. Finally, and most practicably, there is the amount the employee would have to pay for the services in a transaction at arm's length. This is the favoured approach in most countries, including Ireland, although it may be applied in a simplified, standard form to ease the costs of valuation.[11] In Ireland, accommodation provided by the employer is valued on the basis of market rental, whereas company cars are valued according to a standard formula based on the new value of the car and the relationship between personal and business mileage.

Should all such benefits be subject to tax? The answer in Ireland is based on a mixture of administrative compromise, specious argumentation and special pleading. Company cars, employer-provided accommodation and loans from the employer at rates lower than would be payable in the market are taxable as part of the employee's remuneration. Subsidised

---

11 This statement applies to the major forms of benefit in kind. Minor items are valued at the cost to the employer.

meals in the firm's canteen, company crèches, bus/train passes and free car parking are not taxable. The first is presumably excluded because of the costs of valuation, but the others are more difficult to justify. The exemption of crèches is another reflection of the view, discussed above, that it is socially desirable to subsidise people to enter the formal labour force. The transport passes are exempt to encourage people to use public transport (rather than their own cars) to travel to work, but this is an odd way to do it – it might be better to remove the exemption and use the revenue to subsidise public transport – and, in any case, it is contradicted by the exemption of free car parking. There is a widespread view that the tax-free status of free car parking is maintained because civil servants are major beneficiaries.

When a benefit in kind is not taxable in the hands of the employee, a compromise would be to deny to the employer a deduction for expenses incurred in providing the benefit in question. This would be a good substitute if the employer were not a company and so would be subject to income tax, since in many cases the marginal rate facing each party would be the same. Thus, the revenue gained by denying a deduction would equal the revenue lost by not taxing the benefit.[12] This would not be the case for corporate employers since the rate of corporation tax, in most cases, is less than either of the marginal rates of income tax. Also, some of the major untaxed benefits do not give rise to potential deductions since the cost of provision cannot be determined by normal accounting methods.[13] For example, if an employer uses some of his land to provide free parking places for employees, the economic cost is the opportunity cost of that land – something not revealed by his accounts and so not something for which he could claim a deduction. The same would apply to an airline providing free seats to employees. In any case, Irish tax law does not deny deductions for such expenditure and, even where it would be appropriate, the compromise is not used.

Saving and income from saving

There is a long-standing debate among tax economists as to the relative merits of income and consumption as the base for direct taxation. A tax

---

12 This is only approximately true because the normal method of valuing taxable benefits gives a greater value than the potentially deductible cost of providing them.

13 Or, in the case of the author's employer, who provides free parking but is a tax-exempt charity, deductions are inapplicable.

based on consumption (usually called an expenditure tax) is the same as an income tax with a full deduction for income saved or, under certain conditions, is the same as an income tax that exempts income from capital. The debate has hinged on the fact that a comprehensive income tax distorts the choice between consumption and saving – that is, contravenes the efficiency criterion – whereas an expenditure tax has no such effect. However, since an expenditure tax provides a disincentive to earning labour income that is greater than that provided by an income tax (because the rate has to be higher to offset the fact that the base is lower), the issue is then the empirical one of whether the welfare loss resulting from the taxation of saving and work under an income tax is greater than the loss from the taxation of work under an expenditure tax. No firm conclusions have been reached on this matter.

What this debate decidedly does not appeal to is the notion that there is something especially good about saving, something that needs saving to be stimulated by discriminatory tax incentives. Unfortunately, this is exactly the notion to which Ministers for Finance often appeal when introducing an especially favourable tax treatment of saving or income from saving. It is true that an economy cannot grow if it always consumes all current income, because it cannot finance investment.[14] However, individuals have reasons to save for their own purposes (such as future consumption or bequests to children) and it is not at all obvious that society as a whole would be better off if individuals saved more than they otherwise would simply because of the tax advantages of doing so.

Another underlying issue concerns the effect of inflation on income from capital. Suppose one has an asset with a value of €10,000 at the beginning of the year and the rate of return is 5 per cent. There is a potentially taxable income of €500. However, suppose that the rate of inflation during the year is also 5 per cent. The whole of the return is therefore needed to maintain the real value of the asset and so, according to the comprehensive definition, there is no income. Indeed, if the rate of inflation had exceeded the rate of return, income would have been negative. Should the tax system take this into account?

---

14 Even if, in any year, all investment is financed from foreign borrowing and none from domestic saving, that borrowing can be serviced in the future only by not consuming all future income.

In principle, there is an argument for taxing only the real return to capital, but there are practical problems. Suppose the market value of the asset generating the income responded to inflation, as is likely to be the case with physical assets. Then, a capital gain would accrue that would, under the comprehensive definition, offset the point just made. Then, it would be difficult to know how extensive any provision for taxing only the real return should be. Business profits are a return to physical capital, but normal accounting does not, in general, allow for increases in the nominal value of fixed assets. How would one know how much of the nominal return to allow in assessing taxable income? If the process were to be equitable and non-arbitrary, a complex system of annual asset valuation would be required. In practice, this issue is universally ignored because of this kind of difficulty and, in any case, capital gains are almost never taxed on an accruals basis and so any 'over-taxation' of capital income can be regarded as a quid pro quo for the benefit to the taxpayer of restricting taxable gains to realisation. Nonetheless, the basic principle, if it can be made practicable, that tax should apply only to the real return to capital remains valid and we shall return to it when looking at the taxation of interest and capital gains.

The Irish income tax has a range of provisions relevant to saving. Some saving is deductible in determining taxable income, and some income from saving is either exempt or subject to a final withholding tax at a low rate. We will examine savings media in two categories: pension schemes, and a remarkable scheme known as special saving incentive accounts.[15] The central point is that there is no provision applying to saving, or income from saving, in itself; tax treatment depends upon the *form* taken by saving – that is, the type of asset created by the saving.

Pension schemes

There are three stages at which taxation could, in principle, be applied to saving for pension purposes: the saving itself, the income accruing to the asset before retirement, and the pension. If one makes provision by means

---

15 Until 2000, there was a group of schemes operated by life assurance companies and unit trusts under which the income of the scheme received especially favourable treatment under the income tax and the capital gains tax if certain criteria were met regarding the scheme's investment portfolio. These concessions are no longer in operation as regards new business.

of a deposit account, tax is applied at all three stages (although, of course, not to withdrawals from the deposit itself). On the other hand, provision made by contributing to an approved scheme attracts no tax at all until the third stage. Thus, for example, membership of an occupational scheme works as follows. Contributions made by an employee are deductible up to limits set so as to restrict opportunities for avoidance by earners of especially high incomes and to provide a greater incentive the higher the age of the employee. The maximum deduction is 15 per cent of 'relevant earnings' for a person under the age of thirty, rising to 30 per cent for someone over 49 years of age. The maximum relevant earnings for these purposes is €254,000. In addition, contributions by an employer on behalf of an employee are deductible costs for the employer. The income accruing to the fund is not taxable. Finally, the pension is taxable under Schedule E in the normal way, although, on retirement, a person may take up to 25 per cent of the accumulated fund as a tax-free lump sum.[16]

This way of dealing with pension provision is widespread throughout the world, but it can be questioned. The essential features are that the saving itself is not taxed (whereas the comprehensive definition of income would not allow this kind of deductibility) and that taxation is deferred until the pension is paid. Can this favourable treatment be justified according to the criteria of equity and economic efficiency?

Efficiency and horizontal equity are infringed because the form of saving matters. If you put your savings in a deposit account you get no deductibility and no deferral of tax on the income from that saving. The issue comes down to whether there is an efficiency argument in favour of concessions designed to lock people into long-term savings plans. This has already been considered, with the conclusion that that argument, if it is cogent at all, is weak. But there is another possibility: that tax concessions to private pension provision are fiscally desirable when compared with public provision financed by social security contributions.

To evaluate this contention, we start with estimates produced by the Revenue Commissioners on the revenue foregone through reliefs. For 1999-2000, the estimated revenue foregone by the deductibility of

---

16 Essentially, the same provisions apply to anyone who contributes to an approved pension fund, regardless of whether or not it is operated through his employer (for example, where the contributor is self-employed).

pension contributions was employees' contributions €456 million, employers' pension contributions €645 million and retirement premiums paid by the self-employed €170 million – a total of €1,271 million.[17] These estimates (the most recent available) are rather out of date and, more importantly, they are notoriously unreliable.[18] However, we will suppose that they are accurate as approximate orders of magnitude. Also, to ensure that, if anything, they are under-estimates, let us bring them more up to date by treating them as if they related to 2001. In that year, total social welfare pensions (contributory and non-contributory old-age, retirement and widow/er's) were €2,577 million. In other words, the revenue lost from the tax concession to private saving schemes was approximately 50 per cent of total payments on publicly provided pensions. This point is somewhat overstated because the revenue is not foregone for ever: it is deferred until the pension itself is taxed. However, given the young age profile of the Irish working population, the deferral period is very long and so the deferral is very costly.

Whether or not this is good value for money in fiscal terms depends upon what would happen if the tax concession was not available. There could be a reduction in contributions to private schemes and this could lead to political pressure to increase the state pension – but this would, presumably, be largely funded by means of an increase in social welfare contributions, in which case it need not have any implications at all for the government's overall budgetary position. Even if there were no increase in social security taxes, the income tax revenue gained from the abolition of the concession would fund a 50 per cent increase in pensions.

Thus, a concession that is a subsidy to those who want to have a pension higher than that provided by the state scheme is poor value for money for the public finances and so any alleged fiscal advantage is insufficient to offset the clear inequity of deductibility for pension contributions.[19]

---

17 Office of the Revenue Commissioners, *Statistical Report 2001*, Dublin: Government Publications, 2002, Table IT6.

18 This description would be endorsed by those who produce the estimates, the problem being that the PAYE returns made by employers exclude contributions in the statement of wages paid. The estimates are to a large extent guesswork.

19 Of course, private schemes are funded and the state scheme is not, which slightly clouds any calculations based on contributions and payments. However, in a steady state, even a private funded scheme has the financial characteristics of a pay-as-you-go system.

Special Saving Incentive Accounts (SSIAs)

Under the schemes dealt with above, the subsidy to savers takes the form of tax concessions. The system of SSIAs is remarkable (and probably unique) in that the subsidy takes the form of a grant from the state.

The SSIA scheme operated for one year only – from 1 May 2001 to 30 April 2002. To qualify, a saver must have established during this period an account with a recognised institution and must pay into it a regular amount not less than €12.50 and not more than €254 per month. That amount is not deductible for the purposes of income tax – it is like a lodgement to a deposit account rather than a contribution to a pension scheme. The exchequer pays into the account a sum equal to 25 per cent of the amount saved. The full term is five years and, if no withdrawals are made in the meantime, withdrawal at full term is subject to no tax on the contributions of the saver and the exchequer, and to withholding tax at 23 per cent on the interest accrued. There is no other liability to income tax, capital gains tax or deposit interest retention tax (see below). Withdrawals made before full term are taxed in total at 23 per cent, which can create a loss on the amount contributed.

There are many extraordinary aspects of the Irish fiscal system, but this must be in the running for first prize. The scheme is clearly in conflict with vertical equity since the amount of the grant depends upon the amount saved, which in turn is positively related to income (at least up to the ceiling of €254 per month). The only conceivable justification lies in an appeal to the assertion that it is desirable to have fiscal incentives to increase the rate of private saving – an assertion which has been challenged above.

Deposit interest retention tax (DIRT)

Interest paid on deposits in banks and building societies is subject to withholding tax called DIRT at a rate of 20 per cent (in some cases 23 per cent). The most important feature of this is that DIRT is a final withholding tax: the interest in question is not liable to any other tax.

This is a straightforward infringement of the global principle of income tax since it subjects this particular form of income to the lower of the two marginal rates of income tax, regardless of the rate that would be applied to any given taxpayer on other types of income. The result is to reduce the progressivity of the income tax. Those whose income is low enough to have a marginal rate of zero still have DIRT paid on their deposit interest and those with high incomes pay a much lower marginal rate than they would on other income. Since the value of relevant deposits tends to rise with income, the effect is almost certainly a reduction in revenue from the income tax (of which DIRT is formally a constituent).

These objections could be met if the withholding were not final. However, to do this would be to lose at least some of the administrative advantage of withholding. The number of withholding agents (that is, those who have to make returns to the Revenue Commissioners) is minuscule compared with the number of depositors, who would have to make returns if the withholding were not final. How important this is depends on the number of depositors who currently do not have to make returns for other reasons (for instance, those whose other income is solely wages taxed under PAYE).

Although final withholding at the standard rate represents favourable treatment of interest under DIRT, this is balanced by the fact that the base is the nominal rather than the real return to deposits. We have already noted that failure to take account of inflation when taxing interest causes the principal as well as the interest to be taxed. This may not appear to be too serious when inflation is trivial, but it is still a concern because the nominal interest rate on deposits rarely adjusts completely to inflation. At the time of writing, the real return to deposits in banks and building societies is negative, but the tax applies to the (positive) nominal return.

A feature of DIRT is that it does not apply to accounts held by non-residents, and it was this feature that gave rise to the most spectacular example of mass tax evasion yet seen in Ireland. Irish residents set up tens of thousands of accounts using foreign addresses (with one small provincial town having, in its local branches, more non-resident accounts than the population of the town). When these practices came to light, an investigation by a parliamentary committee forced the Revenue Commissioners to launch a campaign that led to the recovery of very large amounts in taxes and penalties. In all the hand wringing over this scandal, no-one pointed out that the whole business arose solely because non-resident accounts were (and still are) exempt from DIRT. The stated reason for this exemption is to discourage capital flight (or to encourage capital inflow), a reason that has little basis in a world where domestic investment can be financed from foreign borrowing and that, in any case, was never subject to empirical investigation. Capital flight is certainly of no concern now that Ireland is a member of the euro zone and the exemption of non-resident accounts can lead to inter-member distortions – which is why the European Commission has been trying to get members to apply withholding tax to cross-border payments of interest. The exemption is a serious defect in the design of the tax.

Finally, although an argument can be constructed in favour of taxing income from capital more leniently than income from labour, such an argument is not applicable here. Only the interest on deposits in banks and building societies benefits from this lower taxation: other forms of income from capital, in general, do not.

SOCIAL WELFARE CONTRIBUTIONS

This is not the place for a review of the social welfare (social security) system in general. Consideration will be limited to the means by which the system is financed. Although the eligibility for most benefits is related to the payment of contributions, and so the latter can be regarded as similar to insurance premiums, the link is quite weak. First, a high proportion of those qualifying for benefits do so, not because of the contributions they have paid, but because they have received credits (imputed contributions) as a result, for example, of being unemployed. Furthermore, the boundary between the social welfare fund and the general exchequer is fluid: sometimes the fund is 'raided' by the exchequer and sometimes it receives payments funded by general taxes. Very importantly, there is no provision for employees to opt out of the scheme: the payment of contributions is compulsory. Thus, in all material respects, social welfare contributions are equivalent to taxes. The focus here is whether the structure of rates of contribution accords with the kind of criteria we have used to evaluate other taxes. There are several different classes of contribution, but the discussion will be based on the class that applies to almost all full-time employees in the private sector (Class A).

Contributions are paid by both employee and employer. Formally, the employee makes two separate payments – pay-related social insurance (PRSI) and a health contribution. The contributions are determined by the employee's wage, but not in the way normal for an income tax. The usual (and the Irish) income tax on wages has a schedule of marginal rates (first €x exempt, next €y at a per cent, balance at b per cent), which applies to all, regardless of one's total wages. Social welfare contributions, on the other hand, apply a separate rate schedule according to total income. The system is based on weekly wages, except that the ceiling above which there is no employee's PRSI contribution is expressed in terms of annual cumulative wages. Table 3.5, which sets out the 2003 rates, is, therefore, in annual terms on the assumption of a constant weekly wage throughout the year. The employee's rate of PRSI is 4 per cent and the health contribution is 2 per cent and these are combined in the table so that 2 per cent means that only the health contribution is payable, 4 per cent means that only PRSI is payable and 6 per cent means that both are payable (the health contribution is not payable by the employer).

Table 3.5: Rates of social welfare contribution for Class A employees, 2003

Annual wages (€)	Employer (%)	Employee (%)	Total (%)
0–14,924	8.50	–	8.50
14,925–18,512			
First 6,604	8.50	–	8.50
Balance	8.50	4.00	12.50
Over 18,512			
First 6,604	10.75	2.00	12.75
Next 33,816	10.75	6.00	16.75
Balance	10.75	2.00	12.75

Two points are of note in this schedule. First, when annual wages exceed €40,420, the employee's marginal rate drops by 4 percentage points, not something which ever happens in an income tax. Second, at the boundary between income classes, the effective marginal rate can be very high. To illustrate, take an employee whose annual wage rises by one euro from €14,924 to €14,925. The employee's contribution rises from zero to €333 (zero on the first €6,604 and 4 per cent on the remaining €8,321). This is a marginal rate of 333 per cent: the employee would be much better off without the wage increase. He would need the increase to be at least €346 for it to exceed the increase in his contribution. Then again, an employee whose wage rises from €18,512 to €18,513 finds his contribution rising from €476 to €847 – a marginal rate of 371 per cent.

For purposes of simplification, these calculations ignore the employer's contribution and also the income tax. The employer's contribution is a deductible expense and so the effective marginal rate depends upon whether or not the employer is incorporated. The employee's contribution attracts no allowance or credit under the income tax. However, this simplification does not seriously affect the point being made because it is primarily the peculiar pattern of the employee's contribution that generates the high marginal rates at certain levels of income.

An important point concerns the effective incidence of social welfare contributions. Some would argue that most of that incidence falls on the employee, regardless of who formally pays the contribution. Thus, if the employer's contribution were abolished, wages could rise by an equivalent amount thereby allowing the same total contribution to be paid by the employee. Similarly, the same outcome would arise if the employee's contribution was abolished and the same total contribution was made by the employer.[20] In the longer term, the labour market would adjust to bring about these effects, either naturally or through the processes of national pay bargaining. Despite this, policy is often framed as if the distinction between the two contributions were of economic significance.

But, whatever the effective incidence, the discontinuous nature of the schedule of rates is worthy of comment. There is a ceiling above which the employee's PRSI contribution falls to zero – no such ceiling exists for the employer's contribution – and there is a separate rate schedule for each income range, which is what generates the very high marginal rates at certain points. If one wishes to retain the concept that this tax exists to finance defined public expenditure, one could still have social welfare contributions that are merely a supplemental income tax, with the features we insist on in an income tax. The existing schedule is not only of dubious equity, but creates major disincentive effects at certain wage levels.

What is the justification for having separate taxes to finance social welfare benefits, rather than financing those benefits from general

---

20 Things are not quite as simple in practice because these changes would affect the income tax liabilities of employer and employee, but the point is valid in broad terms.

taxation? Most countries with a social security scheme have separate taxes (but not all – Australia, Denmark and New Zealand being cases in point), but the rationale for this is far from clear. We somewhat tendentiously call them 'insurance contributions', but the scheme has few of the normal features of insurance. This underlying issue will not be explored further here since it takes us beyond tax policy in the usual sense.

THE TAXATION OF PROFITS

The profits of an unincorporated business are taxed under Schedule D of the income tax and those of companies under the corporation tax. Similar provisions apply under both headings with one spectacular exception: the rate of tax; although, of course, the taxation of dividends applies only to companies.[21]

Tax rates

The profits of unincorporated businesses are taxed as personal income at the normal marginal rates of 20 and 42 per cent. On the other hand, corporate profits are taxed at quite different rates.

Until very recently, Ireland taxed the manufacturing sector,[22] and financial activities in the International Financial Services Centre (IFSC) and all certified operations at Shannon Airport, at a much lower rate than that applying to other sectors. However, this fell foul of EU requirements. In 1991, the non-manufacturing rate was 40 per cent and the manufacturing rate was 10 per cent. Since then, the non-manufacturing rate was reduced annually until, in 2002, it was 16 per cent. 2003 saw the complete removal of the sectoral discrimination, with all corporate profits being taxed at 12.5 per cent.[23]

---

21 As do the technical provisions associated with groups of companies or with the reconstruction of a company's capital.

22 Including activities deemed to be manufacturing, a major example being the information technology industry.

23 There are transitional provisions under which manufacturers in business since before 1998 will continue to be taxed at 10 per cent until 2010 and companies who set up in the IFSC or Shannon Airport before 1998 will continue to be taxed at 10 per cent until 2005. There is a higher rate of corporation tax of 25 per cent applying to interest, rents, profits on certain land dealings and profits in the mining/petroleum sector. This higher rate will henceforth be ignored.

The very marked disparity between the rates on unincorporated and incorporated businesses could provide an incentive to incorporate one's business, but there is no reason to offer such an incentive. However, this will apply only to small businesses (that is, not to the main beneficiaries of the low corporate rate) and there are certain restrictions on closely held companies (see below) aimed at reducing avoidance opportunities through the incorporation of one's business. The big issue is the justification, if it exists, for having a corporate rate so much below the personal rate and so much below what is typical in the rest of the world.

Does the corporate rate matter as long as it is not higher than the personal rate? The answer to this depends upon how dividends are taxed (see below) and how capital gains are taxed in the hands of shareholders. If profit is retained, one effect is to enhance the share price. A capital gain accrues to the shareholder and, under Irish law, becomes taxable when the gain is realised by the disposal of the shares. But the rate in Ireland is only 20 per cent. So, not only is the underlying rate on profit low, but the benefit to the shareholder of profit retention is also taxed at a rate much lower than the potential rate on other forms of personal income. Thus, the total rate (corporation tax plus capital gains tax) on undistributed profit is lower than the higher marginal rate of income tax.

The more obvious question is the impact of the low corporate rate on the level of investment. Ireland's spectacular success in attracting foreign investment is often attributed to the fact that the corporate rate is very low by international standards. Perhaps this is so, but Ireland has major attractions other than its tax rate. It is in the EU and so exports to other member states attract no duties, and it is English-speaking and so especially attractive to American investors. It shares these features with the UK, but has the additional advantage that it is in the monetary union and so there is no exchange risk associated with foreign currency balances held for intra-EU trade. Ireland also likes to claim that it has an especially well-educated workforce – a claim that will be left unchallenged here. Of course, apart from the linguistic point (and possibly the educational one), these factors are not important to firms intending to export outside the EU.

Then, let us look more closely at the low tax rate. Under the typical double tax agreement, the resident country gives credit against domestic liability on repatriated profits for corporate tax paid in the source country

(Ireland).[24] If the Irish operation is a branch, profit earned in Ireland is immediately taxable in the home country – with credit for Irish tax. So, the effective rate is the higher of the Irish and home rates (which invariably means the home rate). Thus, such operations gain no benefit from the fact that the Irish rate is so low: all the low rate achieves is to pass revenue from the Irish to the home treasury.

If, as would usually be the case, the Irish operation is incorporated in Ireland as a subsidiary, the situation is different. Irish tax is payable immediately, but tax is not payable in the home country (that is, the country of residence of the parent company) until profits are repatriated, for instance in the form of dividends. The benefit to the company of Ireland's low rate, therefore, takes the form of tax deferral on the portion of profit not yet repatriated. Any tax deferral is, in effect, an interest-free loan to the company.

To illustrate the scale of this benefit, let us take the example of an Irish subsidiary of an American company that on average defers repatriation for five years and pays 5 per cent on any debt. Corporate taxation in the US is complicated, not least because, first, the federal tax is progressive and, second, most states have their own tax in addition to the federal tax, with deductibility of the former against the latter. For the purposes of the example, we assume that the relevant total US marginal rate on repatriated profit is 35 per cent. If there were no deferral (that is, all profit is immediately repatriated to the parent), the applicable rate would be 35 per cent regardless of the Irish rate, as long as the latter is less than 35 per cent. Five-year deferral at 5 per cent per year reduces, in terms of discounted present value, the American share of 22.5 per cent (35 per cent less the credit for the Irish 12.5 per cent) to 17.6 per cent. That is, the total 35 per cent is reduced to 30.1 per cent – or by 4.9 percentage points. If the Irish rate were 20 per cent (the same as the standard rate of personal tax), the total rate would be 31.8 per cent – a reduction of 3.2 percentage points.

These reductions seem too small to have a serious effect on the fiscal attractiveness of Ireland for direct investment purposes. Even if the deferral period were longer (as long as it is finite), the difference made by a

---

24 Ireland has agreements that provide for crediting with 41 countries: 16 in Western Europe; 11 in formerly communist Europe; 8 in Asia and Africa; and 6 elsewhere (including the US).

corporate rate of 12.5 per cent rather than 20 per cent would remain quite small. However, the example may be defective for two reasons. First, unrepatriated profits raise the share price of the parent company during the deferral period. Thus, the parent's owners reap a reward in the form of a capital gain even before the profit is repatriated, and this gain, if realised, attracts US tax at a rate of only 15 per cent. Second, and more significantly, the profit may never be repatriated – that is, the deferral period may be effectively infinite and the US corporation tax may never come into play.

At first sight, this does not seem plausible. In 2000, total corporate profits before tax were of the order of €25 billion, but net factor income paid abroad, which is Irish-generated profit moved offshore, was €13 billion.[25] This may not sound like infinite deferral, but it must be remembered that this figure does not measure profit repatriated to parent companies – only profit moved abroad. The US parent may, for instance, set up an intervening company in a third country that does not tax residents on their worldwide income. The profit never reaches the American owners, who benefit from the appreciation in the share price, and is used to finance further investments in Ireland or elsewhere.

If this, or something similar, is what happens, Ireland's low tax rate certainly has a significant impact on the net yield on direct foreign investment and so can be expected to influence the level of such investment. Even if it does not happen, our low rate is something we can effectively advertise and it may be that it acts as a trigger in getting foreign companies to consider Ireland as a location. Furthermore, a benefit comes from the absence in the Irish tax system of any provisions relating to transfer pricing, which is dealt with below.

This story has been speculative, but it is important to know more about the mechanisms through which the low rate influences the inflow of investment, because the cost in terms of revenue would be very high if investment is relatively insensitive to the tax rate. In 2001, total corporation tax receipts, with a rate of 12.5 per cent, were €4,144 million. If the rate has no effect on the level of investment, the loss of revenue from not having a corporate rate equal to the standard rate of income tax (20 per cent) was in excess of €2 billion. This is a very high *annual* price to

---

25 *National Income and Expenditure, 2000,* Pn 10367, Dublin: Government Publications, 2001.

pay to attract investment if most of it would have taken place anyway. No-one would claim that the tax rate has *no* effect on investment and so this figure is unrealistically high, but it does illustrate the point that we know almost nothing about the fiscal price we are paying for investment.

Capital allowances

Taxable profits are essentially defined by the normal accounting conventions that record the difference between income and expenditure, although in certain minor cases some expenditures are not deductible for tax purposes, and in others allowable deductions may exceed actual expenditures.

The most significant issue here concerns the treatment of depreciation. The non-financial assets of a business lose value over time (fixed assets such as pieces of machinery wear out, and assets such as patents or licences become obsolete). To sustain the business's capacity to operate, therefore, an annual sum needs to be set aside into a depreciation fund to finance the eventual replacement of these assets. This depreciation is regarded as an annual cost and is always allowable as an expense before taxable profit is determined. Although the Companies Act permits companies and their auditors discretion over the way an asset is depreciated in the accounts, the Income Tax Act does not: that is, the amount allowed for depreciation as a deductible expense (the so-called capital allowance) is defined by the tax legislation.

There are three parameters in any scheme of depreciation: the base, the method and the rate (or the lifetime). For tax purposes, the base is the historic cost of the asset and not the expected cost of replacement; that is, the total allowable depreciation over the life of the asset may not exceed its historic cost. As regards the method, the two most popular are straight-line, which involves a constant allowance for each year of the lifetime; and diminishing-balance, where the annual allowance is a constant proportion of the depreciated value of the asset, with an adjustment in the final year of the pre-determined lifetime to make the total equal to historic cost. The rate essentially determines the allowable lifetime, for example a rate of 5 per cent implies a lifetime of 20 years.

As a result of changes applying since 2001, the basic Irish system is remarkably simple (remarkable among tax provisions not generally notable for their simplicity). For all plant, machinery and vehicles, the rate is

20 per cent on a straight-line basis, implying a lifetime of five years.[26] For buildings, the rate is 4 per cent straight-line, implying a lifetime of 25 years.

For reasons which will be illustrated shortly, the higher the rate (or the lower the lifetime), the more favourable the capital allowance. The Irish allowances are very generous by international standards, where the rate for plant and machinery would typically be around 10 rather than 20 per cent, and the rate for buildings often around 2 rather than 4 per cent. This generosity could well be as powerful as the low corporate rate in stimulating investment – and it applies to unincorporated businesses, which are subject to the normal rates of income tax.[27]

However, this favourable basic treatment of depreciation was apparently thought insufficient for certain types of construction, which were granted even greater favours. A range of activities from hotels, holiday cottages and farms to private medical clinics can claim capital allowances on buildings at a rate of 15 per cent in the first six years and 10 per cent in the seventh year.[28] This is known as accelerated depreciation because the allowances arrive earlier than under the basic system, the result of which is that, over the lifetime of the asset, part of the tax is deferred. Tax deferral is beneficial because interest can be earned on the amount of tax that is deferred. If the rate of interest is 10 per cent, the discounted present value of the basic 4 per cent allowance over the 25-year lifetime is 36.3 per cent of the historic cost, whereas the present value of the accelerated 15/10 per cent allowance is 70.5 per cent of the value of the asset. If the owner is a company paying corporation tax at 12.5 per cent, the present value of the tax saved by the acceleration is 4.3 per cent of the historic cost of the asset, whereas for an unincorporated business paying income tax at a marginal rate of 42 per cent, the present value of the tax saved by the acceleration is 14.4 per cent of the historic cost.[29]

---

26 A car used in a business may be depreciated for tax purposes only up to a limit – €22,000 in 2003 – regardless of the actual historic cost. For taxis and hire-cars, the rate is 40 per cent diminishing-balance, with no limit.

27 Although, of course, the fact that the tax rate is low removes some of the generosity from the capital allowances.

28 Some other constructions such as multi-storey car parks, park-and-ride facilities and student accommodation can get an even better deal.

29 If the discount rate were 5 rather than 10 per cent, the present value of the tax saving as a percentage of historic cost would be 3.3 and 11.2 per cent for companies and unincorporated businesses respectively.

Even more generous is the acceleration provided under a number of schemes, which are scheduled to lapse at the end of 2004, aimed at stimulating construction in certain parts of the country. The two major components of these schemes are 50 per cent depreciation in the first year (and 4 per cent thereafter) for commercial buildings and, even more remarkably, partial write-off of construction expenses incurred by residential owner-occupiers. The acceleration of the capital allowance is worth, in present-value terms, 10 per cent – 5.2 and 17.6 per cent of the historic cost to companies and unincorporated businesses respectively.

Given the comparative generosity of the basic allowances, the economic rationale for this acceleration is a mystery. It is yet another example of the propensity of Irish policymakers to give discriminatory tax favours to causes they judge to be good, even where there is absolutely no evidence that market failure exists. Why should car parks, holiday cottages and private hospitals not be judged by purely market criteria rather than being given fiscal concessions paid for by taxpayers at large? One can conceive of the existence of market failure in the case of the local renewal schemes, but their coverage is geographically so peculiar that one cannot help suspecting that a political motivation is at the root of the policy. A particularly unfortunate feature of the local schemes is that the relief is discretionary, depending on designation by the minister on the basis of development plans prepared by local authorities. This kind of discretion has no place in a good tax system: it makes the whole thing vulnerable to political patronage and financial corruption.

Dividends

The central issues regarding dividends arise because the company is a rather special form of institution. It is a separate legal entity and, in many respects, is treated by the law as if it were a natural person. It may enter into enforceable contracts, have enforceable property rights, incur tax liabilities, commit criminal offences, be subject to regulations enforced by the courts, and sue or be sued for torts. The whole point of incorporation is to create a legal separation between this entity and the natural or legal entities that own it (its shareholders).[30] What is at stake here is the extent

---

30 Above all, to limit an individual owner's vulnerability to be sued with respect to liabilities incurred by the company.

to which, for the purposes of profits taxation, a company should be regarded as separate from its owners.

At one extreme is the stance that a company is legally separate from its owners and should be regarded as totally separate for tax purposes. A company has a tax liability under the corporation tax and the owners have liabilities for any dividends received under the income tax. This is called the classical approach, which has always been applied in the US and, since 1999, has been applied in Ireland. The Irish system taxes dividends under Schedule F of the income tax by means of a non-final withholding tax at the standard rate (currently 20 per cent) operated by the company. The dividend is distributed net of this withholding and, if the shareholder's marginal rate exceeds 20 per cent (that is, currently, 42 per cent), the balance is payable by the shareholder. If the shareholder has an effective marginal rate of less than 20 per cent, the balance is refunded by the revenue authorities. The point here is that no account is taken of the fact that the dividend is paid from profits already taxed under the corporation tax.[31]

At the other extreme is the view that, economically, a company is a fiction: anything it earns or owns de facto accrues to or is owned by its shareholders. The purest form of this would demand the abolition of a separate corporation tax: all the profits of the company, including those retained in the company, should be attributed to the shareholders and taxed in their hands under the income tax.

An intermediate position was adopted by Ireland until 1999 (and is in use currently in many EU member states). Those adopting this position say that the classical approach involves the double taxation of dividends: any profit distributed has already borne corporation tax and this should be recognised when it comes to taxing the dividend when it reaches the shareholder. This provides the basis for the so-called imputation system, under which, when the dividend is to be taxed in the hands of the shareholder, a credit is granted with respect to the corporation tax already paid by the company on the profits from which that dividend is paid.[32]

---

31 The withholding tax is not payable on dividends to certain types of shareholder, for example other companies, pension funds and other entities such as charities whose income is exempt from income tax. It may also not apply under certain international agreements.

32 An alternative, designed to achieve the same objective, would be to tax dividends in the hands of the shareholder, but allow them as a deductible expense for the distributing company.

Some EU members attempt to achieve a similar result by applying a special low rate of income tax to dividends.

Until quite recently, there was a well-nigh universal view among tax economists that the classical approach should be rejected. The double taxation of dividends, they argued: was inequitable as this form of income was being taxed (total of corporation and income tax) more heavily than the same amount of other income; violated economic efficiency because this heavier taxation biased the choices of wealth holders against holding their wealth in the form of corporate equity; and amplified the tax bias within companies against equity rather than debt finance (interest on debt being a deductible expense under the corporation tax, but dividends are not). To illustrate, take a company with pre-tax profits of €100. It pays corporation tax at 12.5 per cent, leaving €87.50 to distribute as a dividend. Under the classical system, this dividend is taxed as personal income at a rate, for most shareholders, of 42 per cent. Total tax is therefore €49.25, whereas under pure imputation it would be €42.00.

There are counter-arguments, but they are not convincing. It used to be claimed that the completely separate taxation of companies (the classical approach) was a quid pro quo for the corporate privilege of limited liability. However, this privilege is of value only to loss-makers, who pay no tax anyway, and we now hear less of this argument. The most prevalent point made in favour of the classical system is that the double taxation of dividends is capitalised in share prices (that is, one buys shares at a price lower than would be the case if the double taxation did not exist) and so the cost of corporate finance is not affected. If the double taxation were removed by the introduction of imputation, all that would happen would be an increase in share prices and so the granting of a windfall gain to those who were shareholders at the time of the change. The gain in revenue from the adoption of the classical approach would have no permanent effect on the cost of capital. This is a cogent argument, but the trouble is that it would apply to almost any proposed change in the taxation of capital income and, if accepted, would be a prescription for locking us into the existing system, whatever its defects.

It is sometimes claimed that it is difficult to apply imputation when the company and the shareholders reside in different countries – a situation of great importance to Ireland. This is true, but it is hard to believe that the difficulties are insuperable.

Now, to consider the other extreme view: that the existence of the company as an intermediary between the profits and the shareholders who actually own them should be ignored and all profits be taxed in the hands of shareholders, not the company. This is, in principle, a most attractive approach, but the problem is how to operate it, especially since account now has to be taken of undistributed profits. A dividend is paid to an identifiable shareholder, but the owners of retained profits are less easily identified. Those on the share register at the end of the year could be the targets, but this would lead to all sorts of distortion in share transactions as wealth holders moved briefly out of profitable companies to avoid being attributed with taxable profits. It would be better to attribute the profits according to the proportion of the year that each shareholder held the shares of the company in question. This would be very cumbersome. Then, the system must find a way to deal with the situation when dividends are paid from reserves built up from previously retained profits (or reserves created by asset revaluations) – that is, profit that may have been earned before the recipient of the dividend owned equity in the company. The implication of ignoring the company and taxing all profit, retained or distributed, in the hands of the owners is that dividends should be free of tax. This 'pass through' approach, under which the existence of the company is ignored, would in practice be complex to administer and, therefore, vulnerable to avoidance.

The imputation system is certainly practicable (it operates currently in many countries and, until recently, in Ireland) and is not vulnerable to the accusation of double taxation that many associate with the classical approach. So, why did Ireland abandon it? In his Budget speech on 2 December 1998 when the change was proposed, the Minister for Finance announced that:

> Since owners of capital in the form of shares will benefit from the reduced rate of corporation tax on profits, it is right that the Government should accordingly take action to ensure that the tax due on dividends is paid to the Exchequer.

The reasoning here is far from transparent. It suggests that the low rate of corporate tax (presumably favoured by the minister since he could propose its increase) should somehow benefit companies and thus attract them to invest in Ireland, but not benefit the shareholders of those companies. If so, it seems to be based on a misunderstanding of how imputation works. If it works properly, the rate of corporation tax is, given the rate of personal tax, irrelevant. A low corporate rate means a low credit for the shareholder and so a higher net rate of income tax on the shareholder. All that happens if the corporate rate is changed is that the proportion of the tax on dividends payable under corporation tax changes, but the total tax on the dividend depends solely on the personal rate. The whole thing is opaque in the extreme and the move from the imputation to the classical system was without justification, unless one believes in the classical approach anyway – in which case it would be better to say so and not confuse the issue with a reference to the corporate rate. If there was a belief that dividends were under-taxed, it would have made more sense to retain imputation but raise the corporate rate.

Close companies

A close company is, broadly speaking, one which is owned by five or fewer persons (or by its directors, who may exceed five in number), although this definition does not apply to a company owned by another company that is not a close company. Because there is a large difference between marginal corporate and personal tax rates in Ireland, intimate association between a company and its owners could give rise to opportunities for avoidance. Therefore, there are restrictions relating to close companies designed to reduce such opportunities. The essence of these restrictions is to limit the deductibility of certain payments by the company, including: certain benefits provided to owners are treated as dividends rather than deductible expenses, as is interest on loans from owners above a certain level; loans to owners are treated as receipts in the hands of the owners and subject to tax withholding by the company; and a 20 per cent surcharge is added to the normal corporate rate for close companies who fail to distribute their profits within a certain period.

Transfer pricing

Transfer pricing refers to the artificial valuation of sales between associated companies. Many jurisdictions have, in their profits tax laws, provisions by which the revenue authorities may re-assess declared profit according to prices that would rule if all relevant transactions had been conducted at arm's length. Ireland has no such provisions, and this could be of great benefit to many of the international companies operating in this country. It pays an international conglomerate to show as much of its total profit as possible as accruing in the country with the lowest tax rate. Sales to, and purchases from, foreign companies operating in Ireland are often between members of a group with operations elsewhere. Ireland's especially low rate of corporate tax therefore provides a considerable incentive for the local company to undervalue its purchases from, and overvalue its sales to, other members of the group. This enhances any investment incentive offered by that low rate and presumably helps to explain the absence in Ireland of transfer-pricing provisions: we gain revenue from it (because the local tax base is artificially inflated) and it is not us, but foreign treasuries, who lose revenue from it (because the foreign tax base is artificially reduced).

CAPITAL GAINS TAX

Capital gains arising in the normal course of business (that is, where trade in assets is the normal business or where the gain arises as a result of disposing of an asset used in the normal business) are, in Ireland, treated as part of business income and were dealt with above.[33] We are here concerned with what are sometimes called 'casual' gains – gains not in the normal course of business. We begin by reviewing some general principles and then evaluate Ireland's treatment of casual gains by reference to those principles.

Gains as income

Are capital gains equivalent to income in their effect on ability to pay taxes; and, if gains are not taxed as income, will there be a distortionary incentive to receive a return to capital in the form of capital gain rather than, say, interest or dividend? Both equity and efficiency are at stake here.

Clearly, the comprehensive definition of income includes capital gains as they accrue, since that definition equates income to the maximum one

---

33 This is a slight simplification. A realised gain is chargeable to the corporation tax if the disposal was on 'trading' account, but to the capital gains tax if it was on 'capital' account. The former would usually apply to gains on stock-in-trade (inventories) and to gains on foreign exchange when it is held, not as an investment, but to finance normal trading activities.

could spend without reducing one's wealth. The kind of distinction once appealed to between the fruit of a tree (income) and the growth of a tree (capital gain) is simply not relevant. So, if equal situations are measured by comprehensive income, the failure to include accrued gains in the base of the income tax conflicts with the criterion of horizontal equity. It may also conflict with vertical equity in that it is an established fact that the proportion of income represented by gains is higher for richer people than for poorer people.

The efficiency criterion is involved because if gains are taxed more favourably than other income, there is an incentive to concentrate one's wealth in assets that provide a return in the form of capital gain rather than recurrent income. Thus, if property rents provide a return below the general rate of return on capital, but landlords can look forward to capital gains in compensation (which would have to be the case since otherwise no-one would invest in real property), portfolio choices are distorted in favour of real property, with no obvious social justification. Similarly, equity shares (whose dividend return is low, but whose prospect of capital gain is adequate compensation) will be favoured over fixed-interest securities, again for no reason justifiable by the efficiency criterion.

Despite these points, it is rare for accrued capital gains to be treated in the same way as other income, and we must look at possible justifications for this.

Accrual versus realisation

The comprehensive definition of income would certainly include capital gains as they accrue, but there would be very severe practical difficulties in implementing this definition in this case. Assets would have to be valued annually and the problems associated with such a procedure are reviewed in the discussion of wealth taxes in Chapter 4. For this reason, all systems with which I am familiar tax capital gains (if they are taxed at all) as they are realised.[34] This solves the main practical problem associated with taxation on accrual, but in turn creates two more difficulties: how to deal with inflation and how to deal with so-called bunching.

---

34 An exception may be financial instruments 'marked to market'.

Inflation

Only if inflation is high does it create problems for the taxation of income in general (or of accrued capital gains), but even moderate inflation raises an issue if gains are taxed only on realisation. Suppose an asset bought for €100 is held for ten years and is sold for €150. There is potentially a taxable gain of €50. But if the general price level has risen by 50 per cent over that period (an annual average rate of inflation of only 4.1 per cent, which is hardly explosive) there is no gain at all in real terms. Should the tax law take account of this?

The parameters of a tax, such as the rate brackets in an income tax, are always defined in nominal terms, an implicit assumption for annual taxes being that there is a single price level for the year in question. If there is inflation during a year, incomes in the early part of the year will be 'under-taxed' by reference to the average price level for the year, and those in the later part 'over-taxed'. This is an acceptable compromise. Similarly, we have also noted the over-taxation of income from capital in the presence of inflation. The problem here is different. We are here confronting the issue that the tax base (realised gains) is an aggregate of gains accruing at different annual price levels. The obvious way to deal with this is to revalue this aggregate at the price level ruling in the year in which tax is imposed – that is, the year of realisation. The best way to do this would be to revalue the acquisition according to the general price level ruling at the time of disposal, using, say, the consumer price index. That part of the gain accounted for solely by a decline in the value of money is then removed from the tax base.

Bunching

In the face of progressive taxation, taxation on realisation rather than accrual creates a difficulty conceptually different from that raised by inflation (notwithstanding the fact that many confuse the two issues). The problem is exactly the same as that raised by year-to-year fluctuations in income. Suppose the effective income tax rate on a marginal €2,000 is 20 per cent and that on a marginal €10,000 is 40 per cent, and a *real* gain of €10,000 accrues smoothly over five years before realisation. The realised gain will attract tax of €4,000, whereas total tax would be only €2,000

(€400 per year) if it had been taxed on accrual. There are three ways out of this, none of which is entirely satisfactory.

First, since the problem arises only if the tax is non-proportional, it disappears if realised gains are subject to proportional taxation rather than to the normal progressive income tax. This is the simplest solution, but it is clearly inequitable. The second possibility is based on the obvious fact that the problem is greater the longer the period over which the asset in question is held (with no problem at all if the holding period falls entirely within the year of realisation). A version of this is 'percentage inclusion', under which the proportion of the gain subject to tax varies inversely with the length of the holding period. In principle, this recognises the problem more directly than the first option and is more equitable, but, to some extent, it is bound to be arbitrary. In particular, the extent to which it solves the problem depends upon the way in which the rate of decline in the proportion of the gain taxed relates to the schedule of marginal tax rates. The third possibility is a combination of the other two. Gains realised on assets held for less than one year could be taxed under the normal income tax, with gains over longer holding periods charged to a separate flat-rate tax.

Capital losses

If a person has a salary of €50,000 and gains of €20,000, the comprehensive definition says that his taxable income is €70,000. By parity of reasoning, a person with the same salary but losses of €20,000 has a taxable income of €30,000. Thus, losses are treated symmetrically with gains. If capital losses exceed other income, the net negative income could be carried forward in the same way as business losses are carried forward under an income or corporation tax.

This reasoning clearly cannot apply if gains are taxed under a separate tax applicable only to capital gains rather than under the income tax. In such a case, capital losses would be offset only against taxable gains, with any balance carried forward.

Coverage

If a gain is exempt, the comprehensive definition of income is infringed and the normal issues of efficiency and equity arise. Internationally, the most prevalent exemptions apply to gains on owner-occupied residences (and sometimes other personal assets) and gains on government securities.[35] Rollover relief, by which a business may be exempt from capital gains tax if the proceeds are used to purchase an equivalent asset, is also common. These matters will be taken up again in our discussion of the Irish capital gains tax, as will be the question of when an asset is judged to be disposed of for tax purposes.

The Irish capital gains tax

The capital gains tax (CGT) applies to individuals and companies at a rate of 20 per cent in Ireland. When the asset on which the gain arises is used in a business (that is, the gain could be regarded as business income), the income tax (for unincorporated businesses) or the corporation tax, as appropriate, applies instead of the CGT if the asset is a 'trading' asset. Broadly speaking, an asset is a trading asset if trade in that asset is part of the normal business (for instance a security held by an investment company or a fixed asset in which the business is a dealer) or, for example, when the gain is on a foreign exchange balance and is kept for the purposes of financing international trade as part of the business's normal activity. These distinctions are important because the rate of CGT is much lower than the higher marginal rate of income tax and is higher than the general rate of corporation tax.

A gain arises when an asset is disposed of for more than it was acquired for. It is important to define disposal and acquisition. A disposal (and an acquisition, which is just the mirror image of a disposal) occurs when an asset changes ownership by sale, gift or exchange. A bequest is not a disposal for these purposes: the recipient is not chargeable to CGT (but may be chargeable to capital acquisitions tax – see Chapter 4) and is regarded as having acquired the asset at the date of death at the market value ruling at that time. The chargeable gain is equal to the value on disposal (net of any encumbrances such as a mortgage), less the cost of acquisition and less any costs associated with the transfer of ownership, such as agency fees.

Up to 2002, the acquisition value was indexed by reference to the consumer price index, but there is no longer any indexation with respect

---

35 Academic readers who collect student howlers may like the malapropism I encountered many years ago where, in this context, such securities were referred to as 'guilt edged'.

to increases in value that took place after that year. This abolition of indexation was a serious mistake: it removed the former protection against one of the defects of applying CGT on a realisation rather than an accrual basis and so made the base of CGT excessively arbitrary.

Capital losses in any year may be offset against chargeable gains in that year or, if gains are insufficient, may be carried forward without limit to offset against gains in the future. An important anti-avoidance device is that gains on development land may be offset only by losses on development land, although losses on development land (does anyone make them?) may be offset against gains on other assets.

A considerable range of gains is exempt from CGT. In any year, the first €1,270 of chargeable gains of an individual is exempt. Gains accruing to institutions exempt from income tax (such as charities) are exempt, as are gains realised by most governmental bodies (though not commercial public enterprises). Also exempt are gains on government securities and state-operated savings media such as savings certificates. Whether gains on state bonds and savings certificates should be exempt is debatable, especially since the interest on public securities is taxable under Schedule C of the income tax. This introduces a distortion in favour of instruments whose return is in the form of capital gain rather than interest – clearly the case with savings certificates, but also with bonds issued at a discount. Since interest rates are now determined by the European Central Bank, independently of conditions in Irish capital markets, the overall fiscal implications of exempting these gains are complex to trace. Also, the globalisation of capital markets means that Irish bonds are purchased by foreign residents and so their own, as well as the Irish, tax treatment of interest and capital gains is relevant. However, for two reasons, the exemption of gilts is probably not important in practice. First, by far the most significant demand for bonds in Ireland comes from pension funds, which are exempt anyway on all capital gains. Second, almost all the yield from bonds accrues in the form of interest, which is taxable, rather than from exempt capital gains: most purchasers buy bonds for income rather than gains.

For the majority of people, the most significant exemption applies to gains realised on the disposal of (their main) private residence on grounds of no more than one acre. This is yet another favour to owner-occupiers, supplementing the favours under the income tax, and the issues are the same (see above). It is inequitable and inefficient (though less so than the treatment of owner-occupiers under the income tax because the stamp duty on house sales acts as an, albeit imperfect, substitute for a capital gains tax). However, the exemption has been capitalised in that its existence has increased the price at which the house was purchased and can be sold. The issues here were reviewed in our discussion of mortgage interest relief above.

The most important issues relating to the taxation of capital gains in Ireland are, first, the fact that a separate tax is imposed, rather than subjecting gains to the normal income tax and, second, that the rate of tax is equal to the lower of the two rates of income tax. Although the CGT is slightly progressive (because there is an exemption threshold), it is, for most taxpayers, effectively proportional because the threshold is low. The case for a proportional CGT has already been noted: it means that the bunching problem disappears. However, it is possible to deal with bunching through a system that relates the marginal rate to the length of the holding period – or, even better, through averaging – and the case for a separate tax is weak. This is especially so given that the Irish approach so obviously violates the criteria of horizontal and vertical equity and economic efficiency. For most relevant taxpayers, the marginal rate of income tax is 42 per cent, whereas the rate of CGT is a mere 20 per cent. This is distortionary in that it favours investments whose return is in the form of capital gains rather than interest or dividends, and it is difficult to think of any reason why society at large would benefit from such a distortion. It is horizontally inequitable because a person who enjoys a capital gain pays tax on it at a rate of, in most cases, less than half that payable by someone who received a wage increase of the same amount. It is vertically inequitable because gains subject to CGT are not randomly distributed across the population: they overwhelmingly accrue to those whose total income is above average.

The abolition of indexation increased the effective rate of CGT and has offset to some extent the distortion and inequity generated by the differential between the nominal rates of CGT and income tax. In some cases, it may have actually reversed the discrimination. However, to have two undesirable features working in opposite directions is not a good way to design a tax. It would be much better to restore indexation and apply a higher nominal rate of CGT.

The low rate of CGT was introduced in Budget 1998 – four years before indexation was abolished – as a reduction from the then rate of 40 per cent. In his budget speech on 3 December 1997, the Minister for Finance stated:

> For a considerable period of time, I have been of the strong view that a reduction in capital gains tax will release pent-up investment funds and create an incentive for the acquisition of further capital assets. This will encourage investment and growth in the future.

That was the total of the justification offered, though it was supplemented on 28 January 1998 by the following answer to a parliamentary question:

> The higher rate of capital gains tax discouraged individuals from placing their capital at risk in new ventures. The 40 per cent rate encouraged the long-term holding of assets, often until death, without regard for commercial considerations. . . . Furthermore, the reduction in the rate of capital gains tax will redress the imbalance which existed between the taxation of risk-free deposits and productive risky investment.

What is to be made of all this? First, where were these 'pent-up investment funds' such that their release from the shackles of a 40 per cent CGT would lead to the 'acquisition of further capital assets'? Under myriad mattresses? Unless it is claimed that the total available to finance investment would increase (if so, why not say so?), the change in the relative tax treatment of various financial instruments would simply lead to a shift in the relative supply of funds to those various instruments. The second quotation throws some light on this issue: apparently, the objectives were to undo any lock-in effect and to shift the supply of funds from less risky to more risky assets.

The idea that a CGT on realised gains may discourage the sale of assets (lock-in) is an old one, but there is no evidence that this effect is of any significant scale (except, possibly, in the case of land needed for residential development). The point made by the minister is really a comment on the fact that Ireland's CGT does not treat a bequest as a disposal. If lock-in until death is a problem, the more obvious response would be to amend the CGT, not by reducing its rate, but by treating bequests as disposals, a solution that has much to be said for it in a country where rates of inheritance tax are low (see Chapter 4).

The effect that a tax on capital income (which includes CGT) has on an investor's choice between more and less risky assets is complex and little is known about it empirically. Given that capital losses may be offset against gains for the purposes of CGT, the exchequer participates in the risk to the extent of the tax rate. Furthermore, if a risky asset is one with a low probability of any given income (dividend or interest), one would have thought that the existence of an income tax with a marginal rate of 42 per cent would provide some stimulus to risk-taking (that is, load the dice against assets whose return would be taxed under the income tax). In these circumstances, a CGT with a rate approximating to the relevant marginal rate of income tax should be neutral with respect to the riskiness of assets. It is, therefore, hard to believe that any bias against risk-taking was serious when the rate of CGT was 40 per cent.

Thus, it is difficult to find convincing the reasons put forward for the reduction in the CGT rate to less than half the higher rate of income tax. The main beneficiaries are those with large holdings in public companies and those who make large profits from sales of development land. The latter is particularly problematic. Development profits arise almost entirely from the re-zoning of land for residential purposes on the outskirts of major towns: that is, they arise because of planning decisions by local authorities. We are now, rightly, concerned about corruption in this area, but we seem to be less concerned at the possibility that the tax system creates an incentive for such behaviour.

4

The Taxation of Wealth

Some may ask, appealing to horizontal equity, whether or not it is reasonable to regard two persons with equal income but differing wealth as being in equal situations when it comes to their ability to pay taxes. Surely, a person with large accumulated or inherited wealth who, having little or no income, lives off that wealth is in a better position than another person who also has little or no income but also has no wealth. Furthermore, vertical equity – or the desire for redistribution – undoubtedly applies to wealth as much as, or even more than, to income. Many would argue that societies are more likely to be unfair because of disparities in wealth (which lead to disparities in power) than because of inequality of income.

The efficiency criterion is also relevant. Some claim that it is desirable that the members of society accumulate wealth and that the favourable tax treatment of wealth provides an incentive to do this – a kind of efficiency argument. On the other hand, it is not obvious that society has any interest at all in the rate of wealth accumulation, over and above the interest of the individuals who engage in the accumulation (because they want to provide for their old age or for their children). Wealth is accumulated by the choice of the individual to save rather than consume. Why should we want to distort that choice? The argument is strong only to the extent that the favourable treatment of wealth is designed to offset some other distortion that works against the socially optimal rate of accumulation. But, even if that were the case, the best policy is to favour saving rather than wealth. This argument could be used to counteract the equity argument, but it is harder to use it for that purpose when it comes to inherited wealth, except to the extent that tax favours to inherited wealth may encourage people to save.

One argument for a wealth tax (in this case as a possible replacement for an income tax) has frequently surfaced in relation to land. If land is left idle or not utilised to its potential, the user attracts no penalty under an income tax. Under a tax applying to the capital value of the land, however, there is an incentive to use the land productively.

There are, therefore, good reasons for considering wealth as a tax base, but there is no denying the difficulties and we review these now.

The definition of wealth

Wealth differs from income in that the former is measured at a point in time (as in a company's balance sheet), whereas income is measured over a period of time. Wealth consists of assets that have a market value because: their ownership confers rights to future income (examples are real property, securities and patents), their ownership generates 'psychic' income or enjoyment (pictures, jewellery and so on), they can be directly consumed (wines or owner-occupied residences) or they can be costlessly converted into consumption (cash). These examples have all been considered as components of the base of a wealth tax, but there is one serious gap in the list.

Take two persons, A and B, that have the same income and consume the same amount. Person A puts his saving into bonds, which generate future income and are directly marketable. Person B puts his saving into improving his education, which also generates (additional) future income but which is not directly marketable. What is the difference? In principle, none. 'Human capital' (natural ability enhanced by education and training) can only rarely be sold as an asset (footballers who get a slice of the transfer fee and high-powered executives who receive 'hello money' would be cases where it is sold), but it does derive from investment and does generate income in the same way as real property or securities. If we restrict a wealth tax to non-human forms of capital, we introduce a bias into the portfolio choices of savers, which violates the efficiency criterion.

It also violates horizontal equity, since the tax system is discriminating among different types of asset of equal value.

There is no obviously practicable way of coping with this problem. We could try to attribute a taxable value to the various stages of education or various types of vocational training, but it would be arbitrary and, in any case, it is impossible to take account of the fact that a person's human capital is significantly influenced by his inherent (inherited?) abilities. Also, certain types of education generate positive externalities: someone who gets pleasure from discussing literature benefits if his investment in education increases the number of persons with whom he can discuss it. On the other hand, I get no benefit at all from your vocational training or your holding of securities.

There are some forms of wealth that would be very hard to tax without inconsistency in the fiscal system. Statistics on the distribution of wealth rarely, if ever, include rights to certain publicly provided goods or income. Take accommodation: this is easy to tax if I own my own house, but if I live (perhaps at a subsidised rent) in contractually secure public accommodation, it would be hard to tax this without contradicting the justification for public housing. The same applies to public pension provisions. The right to a public pension is incontestably part of wealth, but to tax this right would counteract the redistributive point of such schemes. So, although the application of a wealth tax to these publicly provided assets would be required by horizontal equity and economic efficiency (as long as the holding of equivalent private assets were taxed), there are good reasons for not doing this. The potential defects in this approach would, in a typical real-world wealth tax, be dealt with by exempting the private equivalents (owner-occupied houses and private pension rights).

Double taxation?

In reasonably competitive markets, the market value of an asset is equal to the discounted present value of the expected income stream generated by that asset. Thus, if one applied a wealth tax as well as an income tax, one would be taxing the same capital value, or income stream, twice. This does not matter in itself since it just means that the effective rate of income tax or wealth tax, whichever way one looks at it, is higher than it seems. As long as the wealth tax is universal and uniform (and so is the income tax) and capital markets operate so that the taxable rate of return on assets is equalised across assets, no inequity or inefficiency is introduced by applying both taxes. However, the conditions just stated never actually hold. For example, not all assets give rise to taxable income (how can one tax the flow of enjoyment from viewing one's art collection?) and, even when they do, all sorts of factors prevent the equalisation of returns to various forms of capital. To tax both wealth and the income it generates creates inequities and distorts portfolio choice.

There are, nonetheless, good reasons for taxing wealth. First, it is hard to deny that a person who gets an income of €x from government bonds is better off than someone who gets the same income from wages. It is secure from the effects of illness or unemployment. In some countries, this has been dealt with by taxing wage income more lightly than income from capital (this is done currently in Ireland by the granting of a special tax credit for wage income), but it is arbitrary. Second, a person who holds his wealth in pictures pays no income tax on the psychic income he receives, but someone who holds the same level of wealth in the form of securities is subject to income tax because the return is in monetary form. Thus, the absence of a wealth tax can be said to violate both efficiency and horizontal equity criteria (and also vertical equity since holdings of non-human wealth are greater for those with larger monetary incomes).

Practical difficulties

The main practical issues concern the definitional, administrative and political difficulties of applying wealth taxes.

No-one attempts to tax human capital, so we leave that on one side and concentrate on marketable assets. A comprehensive wealth tax requires the periodic (normally annual) valuation of assets. Real property in urban areas is subject to continuous trading and so market values can be, to a reasonable degree of approximation, established objectively. The same applies to securities traded on a stock exchange. Less easy is rural property, which is subject to less continuous trading. Hardest of all are things that are infrequently traded such as pictures or jewellery.

It is barely conceivable that a wealth tax could be administratively feasible except through self-assessment, but this makes the system vulnerable to evasion. Income involves two parties, the payer and the payee, and so audit is possible without too much controversy. The valuation of many assets is much more difficult and non-compliance is too easy to undertake and too hard to detect.[1] As a result of this, no country applies a wealth tax to all forms of non-human capital (still less to human capital). This is certainly a compromise because the strict application of the equity and efficiency criteria requires universality and uniformity in the taxation of wealth. But many would regard this as preferable to having no wealth tax at all.

It must also be recognised that wealth taxation is more politically sensitive than income taxation. It raises all sorts questions such as the alleged social undesirability of taxing the family farm or business, the family home of an aged widow or even the stately home that is part of our cultural heritage.

As a result of their very high collection and compliance costs, reasonably general wealth taxes are much less common than income taxes. Much more prevalent are taxes applied when wealth is transferred through gift or inheritance. The valuation of transfers raises the same difficulties as were reviewed above, but this valuation is much less frequent: it does not have to apply to all assets every year. Furthermore, the legal procedures for establishing the beneficiary's right to the asset (probate in the case of bequest) can be employed by the tax authorities as part of the tax assessment and collection mechanisms. It is also claimed that inheritance or gifts are peculiarly undeserving ways of acquiring wealth (unlike one's own saving) and that inheritance and *inter vivos* gifts are ways by which unfair distributions of wealth are passed from generation to generation. That is, inheritance and gift taxes directly tackle the feature of wealth distribution that many find most objectionable.

The only other common kinds of tax on wealth are annual taxes on real property (in many countries and in a restricted form in Ireland) operated by state or local government, and stamp duties. Local property taxes are ignored here and stamp duties are dealt with later in this chapter. We now turn to the Irish tax on capital transfers.

---

1 A favourite device among tax economists is to require that a wealth holder sell an asset to the first person (the tax authorities?) to offer him the value he has declared for his asset. This could be a powerful anti-evasion device, which has actually been proposed for land taxation, but I know of no case where it has been implemented.

CAPITAL ACQUISITIONS TAX

Taxes on the transfer of wealth through inheritance have a very long history in the form of estate taxes – that is, taxes where the liability is on the estate of the deceased and that liability is independent of the number of bequests into which the estate is divided. Such taxes are usually supplemented with a mechanism for taxing *inter vivos* gifts, by having a provision which states that a gift from the deceased less than so many years before death is counted as being within the estate at death.[2]

The next stage of development is a tax on wealth transfers, by gift or inheritance, the liability being on the beneficiary. Thus, since such taxes are invariably progressive, the total tax payable with respect to an estate, in the case of bequests, does vary according to the number of bequests into which the estate is divided. Such a tax may develop into a partial accessions tax, which involves the aggregation over a beneficiary's lifetime of all transfers received by that beneficiary from one benefactor; the point of this being to remove the incentive for a benefactor to pass on his wealth to a single beneficiary in portions, culminating in a bequest at death. Finally, there is a full accessions tax, which aggregates transfers received by a given beneficiary from all benefactors. As far as I know, Ireland is the only country to have had a full accessions tax – the capital acquisitions tax (CAT). However, since 2000, the CAT has reverted to a partial accessions tax.

The CAT in outline

Since it was introduced in the mid-1970s as a replacement for the death duties that originated in the late nineteenth century, CAT has gone through several changes, but two features have remained in place. First, the familial relationship or consanguinity between the benefactor and the beneficiary influences the effective rate of tax. This is achieved by having different exemption levels, or thresholds, depending upon the class of consanguinity. Second, the base of the tax is defined by the aggregation of bequests and gifts received by a beneficiary. The range of this aggregation has changed over the years. Initially, there was aggregation only with respect to benefits received by a beneficiary from a single benefactor.

---

2   Thus, this provision imposes tax on the optimistic, those lacking foresight and the unlucky.

Then, for a short period in the 1980s, aggregation was widened to apply to benefits received from all benefactors in a given consanguinity class. In 1985, the CAT became a full accessions tax, with aggregation applying to all benefits received by a beneficiary, regardless of the source of those benefits. In 2000, the CAT reverted to a partial accessions tax, with aggregation applying only to bequests and gifts received from benefactors in a given consanguinity class.

Other important changes were introduced in 2000. Until then, the CAT had a structure of stepped marginal rates, the steps and the rates varying by consanguinity class, with the rates applying to gifts being only 75 per cent of those applying to bequests. Now, there is a flat rate of 20 per cent, which applies to both bequests and gifts. The progressivity of the tax now comes solely from the existence of thresholds. The thresholds are indexed by reference to the consumer price index, and the levels in force for transfers during 2003 are set out in Table 4.1.

Table 4.1: CAT thresholds (€), 2003

	Relationship of beneficiary to benefactor	Threshold
Group I	Child, minor child of deceased child	381,000
Group II	Lineal ancestor or descendant, sibling, nephew, niece[a]	38,100
Group III	Others[b]	19,050

[a] If a nephew or niece works for the benefactor and the inheritance or gift consists of assets in the business in which he or she works, he or she is treated as a child of the benefactor. This is designed to reflect common practices in family farms and other businesses

[b] A widow or widower who receives a bequest or gift from a parent of the deceased spouse is treated as a child of the benefactor

Bequests and gifts between spouses are totally exempt from CAT. There is a range of other exemptions covering the transfer of certain assets. If a transfer gives rise to a charge to capital gains tax, this charge is creditable against any CAT liability.

In general, the taxable value of a bequest or gift is the market value, less any attached liabilities (such as a mortgage) and expenses incurred in the transfer. The most significant exceptions to this general rule concern the transfer of agricultural assets (land, farm buildings, machinery and livestock) and interests in private businesses. In these cases, the value for CAT purposes is only 10 per cent of the market value. If the asset is sold by the beneficiary within ten years of receipt and not replaced by another agricultural or business asset, this relief is clawed back.

Major issues concerning the capital acquisitions tax

By international standards, the CAT is quite a sophisticated part of the Irish tax system in that its base is the accumulated aggregate of all transfers received by a beneficiary from a given benefactor. Given that a major justification of a capital transfer tax is to reduce the extent to which concentration of wealth is perpetuated from generation to generation, this fundamental feature is to be applauded. The main defects lie in the highly discriminatory way in which what is basically a good tax is applied – above all, the huge difference between the Group I threshold and the other thresholds, and the 90 per cent discount on market value that applies to the valuation of family farms and businesses.

Of course, capital transfers, especially those within a family, reflect an important component of the social fabric and there is no doubt that the privileges granted to certain transfers under the CAT in turn reflect this. Put another way, whatever the economic justifications sometimes paraded, the concessions result from the extreme political sensitivity of inheritance and gift taxation. So many people think that we should have more or less complete freedom to pass on our family home, farm or business to our (actual or expected) heirs that special concessions are rarely questioned.

Consanguinity concessions

Because of the historical fact that assets jointly used by spouses tend to be legally the property of only one spouse (usually the husband), it is certainly reasonable that a concession be granted to inter-spousal transfers. Whatever the law says about ownership, some assets are in effect jointly owned and, to that extent, what is a transfer according to property law is not, socially or economically, a transfer at all (or at least only one-half of the asset is de facto transferred). This is the capital side's equivalent of the point regarding income-sharing and the choice of tax unit for the purposes of income tax. Those in favour of an individualistic definition of that unit under the income tax should ask themselves whether they would favour a similarly individualistic definition for CAT purposes (which would imply the abolition of special concessions for inter-spousal transfers) and, if not, whether they are being consistent. If, for income tax purposes, the unit is the married couple, it should also be the unit for CAT and a case can be made for the exemption of inter-spousal transfers – or at least some concession.

What is very clear is that it would not be politically acceptable to give no concession to such transfers. Less clear is the justification for the scale of the concessions. A person can give or bequeath an unlimited amount to his spouse tax free. A widower with four children (not that rare in Ireland) can, if the gifts/bequests are equal, dispose of a total of €1,524,000 to those children without the transfers attracting any tax. Is this not overkill? It would certainly go far to explain why the revenue from the CAT is so small.

A less extreme concession, which would seem to deal with the important social issues, would be as follows. Remove the exemption for spouses and apply the same threshold to all transfers, regardless of consanguinity. Then, for a family home left or given to a spouse who was living in that home at the time of the transfer, make the taxable value equal to one-half of the market value, with the restriction that this relief apply to only the first €x of the market value. Other assets that generate an income for the receiving spouse could be treated similarly, again up to a limit. This would reflect the fact that the transferred assets were effectively jointly owned by the two spouses.[3]

Those who think that this scenario is too brutal for surviving spouses should reflect on the fact that the whole point of this type of tax is to limit the extent to which extreme inequality of wealth is perpetuated. The spouse can be reasonably regarded as the pre-transfer owner of half the assets, but that is no justification for applying the full concession to large-

---

3   Similar provisions (though one-half may be too high) could apply to transfers to children who satisfy the same conditions as the spouse (they live in the house and need the income).

scale wealth. A widower may have lived in the bequeathed house all his married life, but it is difficult to support his continued occupation of a mansion with no tax consequences.

It is sometimes claimed that inheritance taxes should be low, especially when there is close consanguinity, because the granting of bequests to one's children may be a major motivation for saving. Otherwise, the rate of saving will be lower. But does this matter? Society either has no interest in the rate of saving or, if it does, the proper instrument lies with the tax treatment of the flow of saving, not the stock of wealth. It is certainly difficult to plead that society has an interest in stimulating saving that will be locked up in luxurious houses.

Family farms and businesses

If capital transfer taxes are justified at all, there is no case in equity or efficiency for discriminating according to the form in which wealth is held. More specifically, farms and other businesses whose ownership is restricted to the successive generations of a particular family are especially prone to inefficiency. Society's interest lies in such activities being opened up to others. Why is it assumed that the children of the existing owners will make the best managers? Such an assumption would be laughed out of court if it were applied to a public company in the form of the chief executive's job being handed on to his son or daughter, which is just what is being encouraged by the concessions granted under the CAT in the case of family farms and other businesses.

Why should society at large, whose tax bills are increased by the concessions at stake here, think that it is better to keep family concerns within the family? It is widely recognised that the market can be defective when it comes to the supply of capital to small and medium-sized enterprises, but CAT concessions are an inappropriate response to this. Furthermore, to favour one kind of wealth in this way is clearly inequitable. Holders of shares in publicly quoted companies are not better off than owners of family businesses with the same market value, and to treat them as if they were is simply unjust.

The family farm has, of course, been an essential component of the social fabric of rural Ireland for a very long time, and it is understandable that massive subsidisation of agriculture – in which tax concessions are only one relatively minor part in a sector dominated by the EU's common agricultural policy – has been employed to sustain this tradition, notably because of a fear that if market forces were allowed to prevail the countryside would be denuded of its population. However, it is perhaps time to move beyond this traditional view. Agriculture is now of minor significance to the Irish economy (the contribution to GDP of multinational pharmaceutical and electronic companies exceeds that of farming), and we are paying a very large price for the subsidies used to sustain otherwise uneconomic rural activities, especially small-scale agriculture. Political considerations may make it difficult to subject agriculture to market forces or, specifically, to implement a CAT that contained no special favours to farmers, but we should ask ourselves whether such favours are supported by anything more solid than sentimentality.

Non-farming family businesses never generated the same resonance in the Irish psyche but when CAT was introduced they were seen as constituting the urban dimension of traditional Ireland.

Liquidity issues

The granting of large concessions under consanguinity provisions or in the cases of family farms and businesses is sometimes justified on the grounds that some of the transferred asset will have to be liquidated to pay the tax. The widower will have to sell his house, the family farm will have to be broken up, and outsiders will have to be sold interests in the family business, all to raise the cash to pay the tax authorities. These heart-rending pleas are completely specious.

Both parts of Benjamin Franklin's dictum that 'in this world, nothing can be said to be certain, except death and taxes' apply here. We may not be able to predict the time of our death, but we can be sure that we shall die and our heirs will be liable for CAT. Knowing this, the potential benefactor concerned about the absence of liquidity to satisfy the tax liability can save an amount to cover the liability. The most obvious, but not the only, way of doing this is through a life assurance policy. If the benefactor fails to do this, the beneficiary can raise the cash not only by selling some of the transferred assets, but by borrowing, using the assets as collateral, for instance by mortgaging part of the farm or real property of the business. Capital markets exist to, among other things, allow wealth-holders to switch from one asset to another – in this case to raise cash on foot of a non-liquid asset that the owner does not wish to sell. Liquidity arguments should not, therefore, be allowed to affect the structure of capital transfer taxes.

Conclusion

The 'reforms' of 2000 not only abolished full aggregation and significantly increased the thresholds, but also changed a tax with three rates (the highest of which was 40 per cent) to a flat-rate tax at 20 per cent – and this is in a system where the highest rate of income tax is 42 per cent and for a tax which already accounted for less than 1 per cent of total tax revenue. The potential value of CAT as a source of revenue and as a mechanism promoting a more egalitarian distribution of wealth is not realised by the current system.

It is known that the Celtic Tiger boom made the distribution of income less equal and, although there is as yet no direct evidence of this, one can surmise that it did the same for the distribution of wealth. By international standards, Ireland's treatment of capital transfers is exceptionally lenient, and it is difficult to justify this. The arguments, from both equity and economic efficiency perspectives, for redistributing wealth through the taxation of gratuitous transfers are even stronger than those for redistributing income through progressive income taxation. The extreme benevolence of the CAT is, therefore, a major weakness of the Irish system.

STAMP DUTY

When assets such as securities or real estate are transferred from one person to another, the change of ownership has to be registered and the relevant documents stamped. The charge for this stamping is stamp duty. It originated as a kind of user charge, paying for public recognition of the change of ownership, but nowadays can best be regarded as a form of capital transfer tax. In revenue terms, stamp duties are by far the most important tax on wealth: in 2001, the revenue from them was seven times that from capital acquisitions tax.

The most important stamp duties are those on sales of securities and sales of real property. The rate of duty on securities is 1 per cent and that on non-residential property rises in steps from zero on transfers valued at less than €10,000 to 9 per cent when the sale value exceeds €150,000. The rate on sales of second-hand residential property is zero up to €127,000 (or €190,500 for first-time buyers) and rises in steps to 9 per cent on any sale whose value exceeds €635,000. With certain restrictions, sales of new residences of an area not exceeding 125 square metres are exempt from stamp duty. Sales of securities issued by public authorities are also exempt.

The duty on securities is low and flat rate and so is unlikely to have much in the way of economic consequences. The duty on residences highlights more interesting issues. First, the stepped schedule of effective rates gives rise to very high marginal rates when steps are reached (the same issue was noted with respect to social welfare contributions). For example, a house selling for €254,000 attracts duty at 4 per cent and one selling for €254,001 at 5 per cent – a marginal rate of 254,000 per cent. This is likely to encourage manipulation of the formal selling price and is quite unnecessary. If it is desired to have a progressive schedule, it can be achieved by having stepped marginal rates as in the income tax.

The second, and much more important, issue concerns the effect of stamp duties on the total cost of housing. If the effective incidence is on the buyer (which is where the formal incidence lies), then the high rates – considerably higher than would be typical in the developed world – could well provide a disincentive to labour mobility, which has serious economic consequences. However, the effective incidence of this tax is far from obvious because of the relationship between new houses, which attract VAT but are exempt from stamp duty, and second-hand houses, which pay stamp duty but are exempt from VAT.

From a buyer's perspective, second-hand houses are good substitutes for new houses, and so one would expect strong convergence between the prices of second-hand houses and those of new houses.[4] On the supply side, the only important influence is the cost of constructing new houses. So, given total demand, the total price, inclusive of any duty or VAT, of a new and a second-hand house will be affected primarily by construction costs (including land).

---

4   Complete equality may not exist because, for instance, older houses tend to be in more convenient locations in cities and so attract a premium, but this premium is not affected by the tax regime.

What this suggests is that there is a close relationship between the duty-inclusive price of second-hand houses and the VAT-inclusive price of new houses, which makes the incidence of either stamp duty or VAT on residences difficult to trace. If the duty on second-hand houses is reduced, the price that can be charged for new houses comes down, thus reducing the profits of builders. Similarly, a reduction in the VAT on new houses will reduce the price obtainable for second-hand houses, the impact being on sellers of the latter. Thus, each of these taxes will affect the prices obtained in transactions to which they do not apply. The impact of the stamp duty on second-hand houses is therefore influenced by the tax regime applying to new houses. One would certainly expect the level of stamp duties to have an effect on house prices (both new and second hand), but the incidence is difficult to measure.

5

The Taxation of Consumption

The main taxes here are value-added tax (VAT) and excise duties. They are treated as taxes on consumption because, although they are (with the exception of the VAT on the retailer's margin) applied prior to the retail stage, the expectation is that they will at least partially be shifted forward in the form of higher prices of final goods and services.

VALUE-ADDED TAX

Although over one hundred and twenty countries have a VAT, and Ireland has had one for thirty years, a brief description of the general properties of this tax is called for so as to minimise the possibility of confusion over terminology.

The basis of a VAT

The easiest way to describe a VAT is to compare it with a retail sales tax. The retail price of a good or service is the sum of the import prices and domestic margins (value added) of the various goods and services entering into the production and distribution chain of the final good or service. The only difference between a retail sales tax and a VAT is that the former taxes the retail value in one lump whereas the latter is applied at successive stages to the amounts that identically sum to the retail price.

In principle, a VAT can be applied to domestic margins in one of three ways. First, each trader could take his margin (that is, sales less purchases of goods and services) and apply the VAT rate to it. This is called the subtraction method. Second, as a producer's or trader's margin is equal to the sum of the payments he makes for factors of production (that is, wages, interest, rent and profit), he could add these together and apply the VAT rate to that. This is called the addition method. Finally, he could apply the VAT rate to his sales (his gross VAT liability or output tax) and subtract from that the VAT he has paid on his purchases (his input tax), paying the difference (his net liability) to the tax authorities. This is called the credit-invoice method because it works by calculating gross liability and then giving credit for input VAT, the documentation for these calculations being invoices. If there is only a single VAT rate, the three methods give the same result.[1] With minor exceptions, VATs throughout the world are based on the credit-invoice method.

In many countries, including Ireland, VAT was initially implemented as a replacement for a pre-existing system of multi-stage sales (or turnover) taxes, which had the disadvantage of cascading – that is, applying tax on tax. Thus, to take the Irish example, a tax was imposed on turnover at the wholesale stage on a range of goods and then another tax was imposed at the retail stage on those goods. The base of the retail tax included the tax paid at the wholesale stage. The result of cascading is that the effective rate of tax on retail sales is influenced by the number of taxable stages through which the good or service has passed, thus producing arbitrary non-uniformity in the effective retail rate. Despite the fact that VAT is applied at all stages, the credit mechanism removes this cascading. It could also be removed by restricting taxation to the retail stage, but this 'all-eggs-in-one-basket' solution makes the revenue more vulnerable to evasion. Also, retail sales involve a large number of taxpayers and it would be impossibly costly to bring the smaller ones into the tax net, which is why all VATs have a turnover threshold. Under a retail sales tax, the revenue lost through evasion or the threshold would be the tax rate times the total sales not captured. Under a VAT, however, the revenue lost is the tax rate times the *margin* (not the turnover) of the evader or the taxpayer below the threshold. The further one goes back in the importation/production/distribution chain, the fewer the number of taxpayers. Therefore, under a

---

1   It would be very difficult to apply the subtraction or addition methods if there were more than one rate.

VAT, where a high proportion of the revenue is collected prior to the retail stage, the smaller number of taxpayers makes the difficulties of control proportionately less.

Furthermore, VAT contains an important element of self-checking. A retailer, say, can claim a credit for tax paid by the wholesaler only if the latter issues an invoice to the former showing the VAT charged, and a copy of that invoice is used to support the wholesaler's self-assessed tax liability. Therefore, collusion between the wholesaler and the retailer is necessary if the tax authorities are to be defrauded. Such collusion is possible, but the risk of revenue loss through fraud is much less than under a single-stage retail sales tax.

Consumption versus production VAT

Under a consumption-type VAT (a C-VAT), credit is given for VAT on *all* purchases, including those of capital goods. It is designed to fall solely on consumption, without falling on investment. Under a production-type VAT (a P-VAT), no credit is given for VAT on purchases of capital goods, and so the tax falls on investment as well as consumption. Ireland's VAT is a C-VAT; as are most.

Origin versus destination principle

Internationally traded goods and services can be treated in one of two ways. Under the destination principle, exports are zero-rated (see below) and imports are taxed: that is, goods and services are subject to VAT in the country of the purchaser. Under the origin principle, exports are taxed but imports are not: that is, goods and services are taxed in the country of the seller.

The two principles have different economic implications, but it is very tricky to know exactly what they are in practice unless the countries in question have identical VAT structures. They most obviously differ in their administrative implications. The destination principle requires border controls so that imports are taxed on entry and exports relieved from VAT. The origin principle does not require these controls, but does require another mechanism not needed under the destination principle: if imports are not to bear both foreign and local VAT, there must be an imputed credit for purchases of imports, otherwise, the local VAT at any post-importation stage will be on a base that includes the foreign VAT. This difficulty represents a departure from the simplicity of the credit-invoice method. Almost all VATs use the destination principle, except where there are customs unions (which seek to avoid border controls for fiscal purposes and where the division of VAT revenue among the members can be contentious).[2]

Exemption

Confusion can arise over the distinction between exemption and zero-rating. Exemption means that the relevant trader is in effect outside the VAT system altogether. He has no liability for output tax and cannot claim credit for input tax. Structurally, the disadvantage of exemption is that it breaks the VAT chain and thus can reintroduce cascading. Take the chain of importation, manufacture and retail, and suppose the manufacturer is exempt. He has paid VAT on his imported inputs, but charges no VAT on his sales to the retailer. He therefore receives no credit. The retailer pays VAT on his sales, but his invoices from the manufacturer show no VAT because the manufacturer is exempt, and so there is no credit available to him. But the VAT paid on the imports is still in the retail price because no-one can receive credit for it, and so the retailer's VAT is paid on a base that includes the earlier VAT.

Almost all countries exempt financial intermediation services from their VAT, the reason being the practical difficulties of applying the credit-invoice collection method to those services. However, most countries exempt a range of activities, often for social or cultural reasons (examples include education, health and admission to galleries and museums). The justification for such exemptions will be discussed later.

Zero-rating

Zero-rating is quite different from exemption. The easiest way to think of it is that VAT is payable, but at a zero rate. Thus there is, conceptually,

---

2   EU member states use a complex system for intra-EU trade that avoids border controls but is designed to achieve the incidence and revenue shares generated by the destination principle. The non-Baltic states that were members of the former USSR use the origin principle for trade among themselves but the destination principle for trade with other countries.

output VAT (which is absent under exemption) and so the seller with zero-rated sales can receive credit for any VAT charged to him on his purchases. An important administrative implication is that a taxpayer's net liability could be negative: he pays no output tax, but has paid creditable input tax. The taxpayer, therefore, qualifies for a refund. Zero-rating removes VAT totally, exemption does not. An entirely general C-VAT is designed to fall solely on domestic consumption and so such a tax would zero-rate exports, and nothing else. Ireland zero-rates a lot more than exports, and this will give rise to some comment later in this chapter.

VAT rates

A country implementing a VAT has to decide how many rates (including the zero rate) to apply. There is no general international practice on this, except that there is a tendency for older VATs (those in Western Europe and Latin America) to have multiple positive rates and newer VATs (in Eastern Europe and developing countries) to have only one positive rate (that is, they exempt some things, may zero-rate others, but then apply just one rate to the remainder of goods and services). Ireland has four positive rates, but only two are of general concern.[3]

There are two major problems with multiple rates (including the zero-rating of some domestic consumption). First, even the formal incidence is not uniform across different consumption items. The putative justification for this non-uniformity is that it is required by vertical equity – goods forming a higher percentage of the budgets of the poor should be more lightly taxed on distributional grounds. This will be examined when we come to the Irish VAT, which has marked non-uniformity. Second, multiple rates significantly increase administrative costs – the law finds itself in difficulties over the boundaries between categories of goods; traders selling goods in more than one category and wishing to be compliant have to bear the costs of categorising their sales and accounting by category; traders less scrupulous about compliance have an incentive to defraud by mis-categorising sales – and the tax authorities have to police all this. Furthermore, the zero-rating of items of domestic consumption

---

3   In practice there are actually five rates: for sales of second-hand cars by dealers, the base is the dealer's margin, not the sales value, to which the general rate is applied. The true rate is therefore the general rate times the ratio of the margin to sales value.

greatly increases the number of traders eligible for refunds – another source of administrative cost.

Major features of VAT in Ireland

Ireland has a C-VAT based on the destination principle and using the credit-invoice method of self-assessment.

Exemptions

The following are the main exempt activities:

- most banking and insurance
- letting of immovable property (other than very long leases)
- medical, dental, optical and certain paramedical services
- educational and childcare services
- passenger transport
- theatres, concerts, sporting events and circuses
- public postal services
- betting
- funeral undertaking.

In addition to the above, de facto exemption applies to those traders who are not obliged to register for VAT. These are farmers, fishermen and those whose annual turnover falls below certain thresholds.[4] The thresholds are €51,000 for those at least 90 per cent of whose sales would otherwise be taxable, and €25,500 in other cases.

Zero-rating

The main zero-rated goods and services are:

- exported and re-exported goods
- supply, maintenance and fuelling of international transport
- human food and drink, excluding restaurant meals, excisable drinks and such items as ice cream, confectionery and crisps
- seeds and plants from which food grows
- children's clothing and footwear

4　Farmers and fishermen are essentially outside the normal VAT altogether and are subject to a special scheme (the so-called flat-rate system). Such a procedure is common in the EU and, despite the fact that several countries do apply normal VAT to agriculture and fishing, is not a matter that we shall pursue here.

- oral medicines
- medical equipment and appliances
- printed books (but not newspapers and magazines)
- fertilisers
- sanitary products for women.

VAT rates

A rate of 4.3 per cent applies to agricultural livestock (excluding poultry), horses and greyhounds. A rate of 10 per cent applies to certain supplies under contracts made before 1993, the most important item being residential accommodation. The only significant 'reduced' rate is at 13.5 per cent and applies to the following main items:

- immovable goods (primarily buildings) and construction services
- heating oil, solid fuel, electricity and gas
- restaurant and take-away meals
- hotels, other holiday accommodation and certain tourism services
- museums, art galleries, cinemas and fairgrounds
- newspapers and magazines
- car hire
- agricultural and veterinary services
- live poultry
- works of art and antiques
- photographic services.

All other taxable transactions bear a rate of 21 per cent.

The treatment of housing

The treatment of residential accommodation is one of the more difficult issues in the design of VATs. Distortions could arise from two main sources. First, in the housing market, new residences are in competition with old ones. If new residences are taxed (as they are in Ireland, at 13.5 per cent), what does one do about sales of residences constructed before VAT was introduced? There are various possible ways of dealing with this (such as imposing VAT on the first sale of any residence after the introduction of the tax), but the Irish method is to impose a separate tax (stamp duty, at a rate much lower than the VAT on new residences) on sales of second-hand residences (but not new ones). This is unsatisfactory in that residences first sold after the introduction of VAT will, on subsequent sale, have paid both taxes, whereas new ones pay only VAT.

Second, residences for rental are in competition in the housing market with those for owner-occupation. In principle, the best way of eliminating distortion would probably be to tax all sales of residences (both new and second hand), tax both actual rents and the imputed rents of owner-occupiers, and give credit for the VAT on purchases to both landlords and owner-occupiers. This gives rise to practical difficulties (estimating imputed rents and having to deal with a vast number of owner-occupiers who are not registered for VAT) and the Irish solution (which is very common) is to tax all new residences, whether for rental or owner-occupation, and then to exempt rents. Thus, exemption for rents can be justified as a contribution to uniformity.

Non-uniformity

The Irish VAT is extremely non-uniform, not only in relation to basic principles, but also by international standards (although the British VAT rivals it in this respect). Large components of domestic consumption are zero-rated, the exemption list is long, and there is more than one positive rate. Less than one-half of the consumption of the average household is subject to the general rate of 21 per cent, one-sixth of it is zero-rated and a further one-sixth is exempt.

When VAT was introduced, it was designed to replace two existing turnover taxes in such a way that the effective rate on most items remained unchanged. There was a wholesale tax on a small range of items such as consumer durables and a retail tax on certain other items, with an overlap between the two. A high proportion of consumption was subject to neither of these taxes. As a result, VAT was very non-uniform when introduced; and it has stayed that way.

Whatever the history, the continuing concern is with the regressivity (with respect to income) of a uniform consumption tax. This is a proper concern, but the issue is whether non-uniformity in consumption taxation is an appropriate instrument of redistribution, especially since that feature greatly increases compliance and collection costs and violates the criterion of economic efficiency.

In general, the progression of rates (from zero through exemption to 21 per cent) does seem to apply to goods and services of decreasing levels of necessity, but some of the fine distinctions are almost comical. Thus, to take a mere handful of examples, a digestive biscuit pays 13.5 per cent, but a chocolate digestive pays 21 per cent; a fruit loaf is zero-rated if the fruit weighs less than 10 per cent of the flour, but pays 13.5 per cent otherwise; potato-based savouries pay 13.5 per cent, but cereal-based savouries pay 21 per cent; circuses are exempt, but fairgrounds pay 13.5 per cent; sheep pay 4.3 per cent, but poultry pay 13.5 per cent; theatres are exempt, but art galleries pay 13.5 per cent; books are zero-rated, but periodicals pay 13.5 per cent; and so on. And what is so special about jockeys and photographers that their services pay only 13.5 per cent? This kind of thing is just a nonsense, probably reflecting random pressures from certain interest groups or the confused views of policymakers as to what is good or not so good for us, rather than any coherent approach to dealing with potential regressivity.

A priori, one would not expect consumption taxes to be very effective in redistributing real spending power because almost all goods and services have a positive income-elasticity of demand: that is, there are very few goods or services on which expenditure actually falls as income rises. Thus, the higher your income, the greater the benefit you receive, in absolute terms, from zero-rating, exemption and reduced rates. Whether or not these give more benefit in relative terms, and so affect conventional measures of income distribution, is an empirical matter, and we now turn to this.

The incidence of Irish VAT

The Appendix sets out estimates of the way the current VAT impacts on different income groups and, then, of the equivalent impact of an almost uniform VAT designed to raise the same amount of revenue. The current, very non-uniform VAT is almost proportional with respect to consumption and only slightly regressive with respect to income. A hypothetical VAT that would zero-rate no consumption, exempt only banking and insurance and apply a single rate to everything else (at a rate of 14.1 per cent compared with the current general rate of 21 per cent) would be somewhat more regressive than the current tax with respect to both consumption and income.

What these estimates indicate is that the extreme dispersion of Irish VAT rates across the various components of consumption does remarkably little to improve vertical equity, particularly when compared with a VAT that applies a single rate to all consumption other than what has to be exempt in a tax using the credit-invoice methodology. This structural simplification would, in terms of disposable income, add 2.5 percentage points to the burden on the poorest 10 per cent of households and subtract 1 percentage point from the burden on the richest 10 per cent. This effect is trivial (and even then is probably overestimated) compared with the offsetting progressivity in direct personal taxes. Thus, the figures shown in the *Household Budget Survey* indicate that the effective rate of income tax and social insurance contributions is 24 percentage points higher for the richest compared with the poorest households. If Ireland moved to a uniform VAT, the slightly increased regressivity could be entirely removed by very minor changes in income and social security taxes.

The case in equity for the kind of complex VAT current in Ireland is therefore very weak compared with the costs of complexity. The general rate (21 per cent) has to be high to make up for the revenue lost through zero-rating, exemption and the application of a reduced rate.[5] In addition, the great variation in effective rates across the different items of consumption certainly violates the economic efficiency criterion. Finally, and very importantly, the current complexity significantly increases administrative costs, both for the revenue authorities and compliant taxpayers. The case for simplification is, therefore, very strong. If this fact was more widely appreciated, we might see the end of the type of political opportunism that caused, in 1982, the fall of a government that had proposed to impose VAT on children's clothes and shoes. Such political opportunism is showing signs of rearing its head again as the European Commission makes noises about bringing Ireland's VAT more into line with that in other EU member states.

EXCISE DUTY

Excises are special taxes applied to transactions involving particular goods and are levied at importation or the place of domestic manufacture as relevant. They are among the oldest forms of taxation currently in force

---

5   Despite having the fourth highest general rate in the EU, Ireland ranks tenth in terms of VAT revenue as a proportion of GDP.

and exist in almost every country in the world. The distinguishing feature is that excises are not a general consumption tax, but (usually) are intended to be a supplement to such a tax in specified cases. They are typically levied on tobacco, alcoholic (and sometimes soft) drinks, petroleum products and road vehicles, and many countries also levy them on 'luxury' goods such as jewellery. Like VAT, but unlike customs duties, they do not discriminate formally between imports and domestic manufactures.[6] They do not apply to exports. Tax rates are typically expressed either *ad valorem* – that is, as a percentage of the import or manufacture price – or *specific*, where the tax is an amount of money per unit volume of the good.

Excise duties form an extremely important part of the Irish tax system. They account for around one-seventh of tax revenue, which is more than either the corporation tax or social welfare contributions and nearly two-thirds of VAT. Despite the importance of these duties, they receive remarkably little attention in public debate or in the professional literature. Perhaps they are simply taken for granted (the media describe them as 'the old reliables' on Budget day) and consumers accept them as fatalistically as they accept the weather. Organisations representing sellers annually make ritual protests, but no-one pays much attention.

Issues

Earlier in this chapter, when reviewing the VAT, we made a case for uniformity in consumption taxation. If that case were completely general, excises should not exist. Therefore, if excises are to be acceptable, a special case has to be made for them, and we now attempt that.

First, excises may be justifiable in terms of economic efficiency. Tobacco, alcoholic drinks and petroleum products are known to have quite low price-elasticities of demand in the short run.[7] Thus, economic

---

6   They may discriminate effectively in the sense that countries often have especially low (or zero) excises on typically excisable products of which domestic production is significant but imports trivial. Thus, France has zero excises on wine and oil producers have low excises on petroleum products.

7   Tobacco is addictive and the low price-elasticity of alcohol relates to a mixture of addiction (for some) and the importance of this product as a complement to social activity (for most). Petroleum products are useless on their own: they are always used in combination with capital equipment (vehicles, heating systems etc.) which have very low rates of substitution in the short run.

efficiency would sanction especially high tax rates on these products. This argument, however, is weaker in relation to vehicles, for which the price-elasticity of demand is not particularly low. Furthermore, there are other products with low price-elasticities to which excises are typically not applied, for example salt and toilet paper.

Second, low elasticities of demand make these products ideal revenue targets because the volume of consumption remains high even in the face of tax-induced price increases.

Third, it is claimed that the goods typically excised (tobacco, alcohol, petroleum and road vehicles) generate negative externalities and so consumption should be discouraged. A negative externality (or external diseconomy) exists when the consumption of an item creates costs for others who are not parties to the transaction in question. The market will not, therefore, operate in such a way as to allow these extra costs to be taken into account when consumption decisions are made, and so the level of consumption of these items exceeds what is socially optimal. The consumption of tobacco creates, on average, health costs for the user and for others (through the effects of passive smoking). Alcohol, to a lesser extent perhaps, has similar effects (including the social effects of alcoholism). Vehicle use creates pollution and congestion, and non-vehicular use of petroleum products creates pollution, the costs of which are not borne by those using the product.

In principle, these arguments seem strong, but we should not overstate them. Thus, if the smoker pays for his own healthcare if he becomes ill as a result of smoking, the existence of an externality is problematic, except with respect to passive smoking. It is not good enough to retort that society would need to put fewer resources into the treatment of smokers and so would have more to devote to other types of consumption, because exactly the same could be said about anything. Then, most congestion costs are borne by other road users: I may increase congestion by using my car, but I suffer from the congestion caused by others and so those costs are internalised and are not externalities at all.

Although externalities may provide a rationale for the imposition of special taxes on particular items of consumption, they give no guidance as to the proper level of those taxes. Efforts have been made to estimate the external effects of the consumption of tobacco and so forth, but they are controversial and there is no evidence at all that, in any country, rates of excise have been set to reflect estimates of the scale of externalities. Thus, excise revenue in Ireland is at a level equal to just over 4 per cent of GDP. Is there any reason to believe that the relevant external costs amount even approximately to that proportion of GDP? Of course not: the rates of excise have little economic rationale, having been set for revenue purposes at politically tolerable levels.

Although their revenue capacity is a traditional argument for excises, that argument is not obviously consistent with the argument based on externalities. The former relies on the low price-elasticity of demand for the relevant goods, whereas the latter, in one form anyway, is seriously weakened if those elasticities are low. It depends upon how one frames the point about externalities. Are excises designed to discourage consumption of the good in question? If so, a low price-elasticity is a disadvantage. On the other hand, excises may be justified, not directly as a disincentive to a particular behaviour, but simply as a way of making the relevant consumers pay the social costs of their behaviour. If this is the argument, then the price-elasticity is not germane.

One argument for excises is that their administrative costs are much lower, per euro collected, than those of almost any other tax. They are not collected at the retail level, but on importation or domestic manufacture. The typical targets of excises are, in all countries, imported or produced in highly monopolistic markets, with a very small number of taxpayers.

Finally, the question arises as to whether rates should be specific or ad valorem. If the excise is primarily seen as a response to externalities, the specific approach is indicated since the scale of externalities is related to the volume and not the value of the relevant consumption. You do not increase health risk by smoking expensive cigarettes or by drinking a given volume of alcohol in an expensive form. Indeed, cheaper brands of cigarettes can in some instances be more dangerous, as can cheaper drink. Furthermore, ad valorem duties have the disadvantage that they magnify fluctuations in both revenue and retail prices if the value of the base is volatile – a point of particular significance in the case of petroleum products. The main disadvantage of specific rates is that, unless those rates are adjusted frequently, the real value of the duty is eroded by general inflation.

Irish excise duties

Currently, excises are levied on four groups of product: alcoholic drinks, tobacco products, petroleum products and motor vehicles. The first three groups are taxed at specific rates, with a mixture of specific and ad valorem rates applying to cigarettes. Vehicles, under a levy formally known as vehicle registration tax, are taxed primarily at ad valorem rates. Excise rates are extremely complex, with fine distinctions within each category of product, but an impression can be gained from the selection of products listed in Table 5.1.

Table 5.1: Excise as a percentage of retail price, 2003*

Product	%
Beer (Heineken in can)	26
Whiskey (Power's Gold Label)	44
Table wine (Price €10)	21
Champagne (Price €40)	10
Cigarettes (Silk Cut)	21
Unleaded petrol	44
Diesel	38
1300cc car (Toyota Yaris)	23
2400cc car (Toyota Camry)	27

* Drink prices were sampled at a shop at the higher end of the market; car prices are based on the list price at a main dealer; cigarette and petroleum prices vary little among (legitimate) outlets

Given the rationale for specific rates, comparisons of ad valorem rates have limited value, but the pattern does invite questions if not comment. Thus, if one accepts that cigarettes are dangerous, one might expect them to be taxed at a rate that has a very large impact on price. However, the rate is lower than on beer, most of the consumption of which has no deleterious effects on the health of either the drinker or others. Perhaps the reason is that cigarettes are especially vulnerable to smuggling, which constrains the duty level.[8] Or perhaps there is an equity concern here, with some evidence

---

8   Some observers believe that, in terms of value, the most smuggled good in Europe is not heroin, cocaine or cannabis, but cigarettes.

that tobacco actually has a negative income-elasticity of demand. In the drinks category, champagne is taxed more lightly than table wine (and for both of these the ad valorem rate would be even lower if we had not taken the duty at the cheaper end of the range), and both are taxed at a markedly lower rate than beer – there is no sign of any concern for equity here.

If the justification for excises is to capture pollution effects, why is diesel taxed more lightly than unleaded petrol? After all, the former creates a higher volume of harmful emissions than the latter. And why is the vehicle registration tax a function of engine capacity? It cannot be related to polluting emissions since these are a function of fuel consumption, which should be dealt with by the petroleum excise. If it is congestion externalities that are relevant here, it is body size, not engine capacity, which should determine the duty.

It must be concluded that excise rates in Ireland have no coherent rationale at all. They are what they are because, in the dim and distant past before anyone had heard of externalities,[9] arbitrary rates were struck for revenue reasons and, subsequently, additions have been made when (politically) relatively harmless methods of revenue enhancement were necessary.

---

9   Although there was probably a notion on the part of policymakers that liquor was bad for the workers. We have passed tactfully by the idea that excises are sin taxes.

6

Conclusions

THE CURRENT SYSTEM

A dominant theme of this book has been the lack of neutrality within the Irish tax system. There is discrimination among different sources of income under the income and corporation taxes; between receipts taxable as capital gains and those taxable as income; among different uses of income, as manifest in selective deductions for saving and non-business expenses; among different types of wealth transfer; and among consumption items under the value-added tax and excises. This chapter brings together some of the comments made in the preceding chapters on these issues.

As regards the taxation of income and capital gains, the concessions in question can all be characterised as rewarding (and so providing an incentive to) certain forms of activity and they invite the following question: do the incentives actually work? And more specifically, does the concession actually stimulate approved activity that would not have taken place in the absence of tax favours? If the answer to this is positive, then the concession can be justified only if there are cogent social reasons for distorting personal and business decisions in favour of the relevant activity. It must be noted that, even in this case, there is a loss of revenue because there has been a diversion of resources away from activity the return to which would be taxable. If the answer is negative, then the revenue lost through the concession constitutes a pointless subsidy, which is financed by taxes elsewhere being higher than would otherwise be necessary. Given the fact that these other taxes carry efficiency costs, the question arises as to whether or not the concession is good value for money.

Let us look first at certain reliefs granted under the income tax for non-business income. The annual *Statistical Report* of the Revenue Commissioners contains estimates of the revenue foregone as a result of reliefs. A selection of the larger items for the tax year 1999-2000 (the latest available at the time of writing) is presented in Table 6.1. Although they are large in terms of revenue foregone, personal allowances are ignored because they are a basic feature of any income tax that is intended to be progressive. The other large item omitted is pension contributions. As noted in Chapter 3, the Irish system is not unusual in the way it treats pension contributions and a good case can be made for exempting income saved, the main issue being that it is only this form of saving that attracts this treatment. In 1999-2000, there were no tax credits – that is, all reliefs were in the form of allowances (or exemptions).

Table 6.1: Revenue foregone by selected reliefs, 1999-2000

Relief	Revenue foregone (€m)	As % of potential revenue
PAYE allowance	354	3.4
Medical premiums and expenses	125	1.2
Mortgage interest	158	1.5
Exemption of child benefit	127	1.2
TOTAL	764	7.4

Source: Office of the Revenue Commissioners, *Statistical Report 2001*, Dublin: Government Publications, 2002, Table IT6

The same report gives income tax revenue for calendar years. If these figures are adjusted to the tax year, the estimate for net revenue from income tax in 1999-2000 is €8,286 million. If the reliefs shown in Table 6.1 (in terms of potential revenue foregone, the proportion shown in the final column) had not existed, revenue would have been €10,321 million.

The reliefs identified in Table 6.1, costing the exchequer over three-quarters of a billion euro, were the subject of comment in Chapter 3. In principle, they can all be expected to have some effect on behaviour. The exemption of child benefit reduces the cost of maintaining children and so could influence procreative or consumption behaviour. One may speculate that, for some, child benefit itself provides an inducement to have children, but it is hard to believe that this effect is significant and it is even harder to believe that the effect of the exemption (which increases what would otherwise be the net benefit by a proportion depending on the marginal tax rate) really changes behaviour. What it certainly does do is make the distribution of disposable income less equitable since it is worth more the higher the marginal tax rate.

The PAYE allowance (now a credit) reduces the effective rate of tax faced by someone contemplating entering the formal labour force, which is certainly desirable from the viewpoint of economic efficiency since the very existence of the income tax distorts the choice between paid and unpaid work. It also improves equity, since the benefit as a proportion of pre-tax income falls as income rises because the credit is a fixed amount and because the relative significance of wages in total income falls as total income rises.

The medical relief appears to reduce the effective cost to the taxpayer of being ill or insuring against illness; and mortgage interest relief appears to reduce the cost of borrowing for housing purposes. But do they really have these effects? The medical relief raises the demand for health insurance and for medical services because the exchequer bears some of the cost. Why should the effect of this enhanced demand not be to increase premiums and the fees charged by doctors and hospitals?[1] Thus, at least some of the benefit of the reliefs may be shifted to the suppliers of the services, the purchase of which has been subsidised. Even if this did not happen, these concessions reduce the progressivity of the system (because more is spent on both medical insurance and medical services as one gets richer) and it is not obvious that society at large obtains any benefit if people spend more on these things.

The same issue arises with mortgage interest relief. Although this concession is now much smaller than it used to be, it still contributes to the excess demand for housing manifested in the rapid increase in house

---

1   After all, no-one would be surprised to receive a higher quote from a garage if the work is to be paid for under an insurance policy. It could be said that hospitals are garages that mend people.

prices. In Ireland, one of the reasons why it is expensive to buy a house is that it is cheap to own one, there being no property taxes (rates) on residences and the exchequer (or, rather, taxpayers who do not have a mortgage) pays some of the mortgage interest. This subsidised ownership raises the demand for housing, to the benefit of builders, landowners and mortgage lenders. Again, there is shifting of the benefit of the relief. And all this when the concession breaches the principle that expenses should be allowed only against taxable income, increases the proportion of the nation's resources that go into housing and distorts the choice between owner-occupation and rental at no clear benefit to society.

We do not know how much revenue is foregone as a result of the facts that certain personal income is exempt (such as in the case of artists) and that DIRT is a final withholding tax at the standard rate. Nor do we know whether those benefiting from the exemptions would have behaved differently (that is, lived abroad) in the absence of the concessions. If they would, we have lost no revenue but have gained their presence, but it is far from clear what sort of gain that is. If they would not, we have lost revenue to no purpose. Either way, we lose horizontal equity and incur additional administrative costs.

If one is convinced by arguments that a comprehensive income tax is inherently biased against income from capital, the DIRT provision could be justified as a contribution to economic efficiency. Also, certain other savings media are favoured and the favour contained within DIRT helps to remove discrimination among savings media. What can be confidently asserted is that the exemption from DIRT of non-resident accounts has no merits at all in that it encourages evasion and conflicts with horizontal equity.

There are no usable figures on the cost of reliefs against business income. The cost of capital allowances is quantified by the Revenue Commissioners; however, the bulk of this is not a concession, but the application of the basic principles of depreciation. It is not known how much revenue is foregone as a result of the accelerated depreciation granted to certain types of construction (see Chapter 3). What can be said is that there is no evidence that these concessionary schemes (car parks, tourist accommodation, town centres, among others) provide any benefit to anyone other than those who are able to avail themselves of them. That is, there is no evidence that the pattern of investment would have been inferior if simple market forces, undistorted by special tax concessions, had determined the relevant decisions. If this is so, these concessions are simply subsidies to certain developers with no quid pro quo for society. If it is not so, and the pattern of investment has been influenced, the question is whether there is any reason to believe that the resulting pattern is socially superior to what would have otherwise happened. Why should we want more car parks than undistorted market signals would produce?

The most spectacular concession to business income is the very low rate of corporation tax. No-one can doubt the contribution that the high rate of corporate investment in recent years has made to Irish prosperity: the question is the extent to which this investment, especially by foreign firms, can be attributed to the low tax rate on profits. If the tax rate is of little significance, all we have done is to transfer money from Irish taxpayers to the treasuries of other countries. On the other hand, the low rate may well stimulate investment; however, to be confident that we are getting good value for money, we need to gain a better understanding of how this happens.

The non-uniformity in the VAT has little to commend it. The high proportion of consumption that is zero-rated, exempt or subject to the reduced rate creates a large loss of revenue – or causes us to require, by world standards, a high general rate in order for the VAT to generate the kind of revenue typically looked for from such a tax. The non-uniformity substantially adds to administrative costs and empirical investigation indicates that it does little for vertical equity in that a revenue-neutral change to a uniform VAT would add so little to the regressivity of the tax that the effect could be easily offset by very small changes in income tax and/or social welfare benefits.

Wealth taxes are very weak in Ireland. We are peculiar among developed countries in applying no property tax (rates) to residences, and our capital acquisitions tax has such a high threshold as regards bequests and gifts to close family, and such a generous treatment of family farms and firms, that revenue is negligible (well under 1 per cent of total tax revenue). The contribution that such a tax could make to both revenue and vertical equity is, therefore, surrendered by provisions that have little economic or social justification.

As a result of exemptions, special concessions and multiple rates, the Irish tax system is extremely non-uniform and extremely complex – with adverse effects on both efficiency and equity. The complexity raises administrative costs, especially for the tax authorities, and therefore more resources are required to enable the system to work as the legislature intended. It also enhances the incentives to evade because the more complex the system the more opportunities there are for evasion and the lower the risk of detection. All the cases of evasion publicly identified in Ireland in recent years have arisen because of the opportunities offered by complexity. Complexity also erodes equity, because it takes highly paid and skilled professional advice to spot the opportunities for tax-minimisation offered by special provisions. Only the rich can afford such advice. This in turn erodes general confidence that the tax system is fair, which undermines compliance.

All this could be a price worth paying if the complexity brought economic and social benefits. Much of this book has been devoted to advancing the proposition that such benefits typically do not accrue from the maze of special provisions that pervades our tax system.

The Influence of the European Union

A country chooses its own tax system, but it will often be constrained by membership of international organisations. Thus, membership of the World Trade Organisation restricts taxation of international trade, but by far the most significant potential source of constraint for Ireland is the European Union. The requirements of the EU have already affected Irish taxes: we have abolished customs duties on intra-Community trade; we were obliged to adopt the VAT when we joined in 1973; we were obliged to eliminate the exemption of export profits from corporation tax; there are some restrictions on the taxation of capital; and we are subject to certain limits on rates of VAT and excises. And we shall certainly be subject to continuing pressure from Brussels as part of EU-wide efforts to bring more uniformity among national tax systems (what used to be called 'harmonisation', and now tends to be given the less threatening label of 'co-ordination').

Economically, these pressures arise from a desire to apply the neutrality prescription implied by the application of the efficiency criterion at an international level. We have already seen this in the adoption of free intra-Community trade. Import duties distort the relative prices of imports and domestically produced goods and we agreed to abolish them. The future pressures will arise from analogous considerations applying to a much wider range of taxes.

Tax co-ordination is important because tax bases are mobile. For consumption taxes such as VAT and excises, bases are mobile because of international trade in goods and services. For taxes on factor incomes such as personal and corporate income taxes, the issue arises because factors (especially, but not only, capital) increasingly migrate across national borders. So, while the abolition of customs duties has removed much of the distortion of consumption choices (although differences in VAT and excises can still affect where one does one's shopping), the existence of differences in income taxes may influence the location choices of firms and workers within the EU. The idea of a common internal market, therefore, implies much more than the abolition of direct fiscal influences on trade and this is why the European Commission continues to press for more uniformity among member states.

Noises have already been made about the extent of zero-rating in the Irish VAT, but these are not really important. Because of the use of the destination principle in the VAT, there is nothing much to be gained by insisting on common rates among EU member states. Countries with common land borders have some interest in this because of the possibility of cross-border shopping (personal shoppers are taxed on the origin principle), but this is of little concern to Ireland. Where cross-border shopping is feasible, the evidence suggests that it is not differences in VAT which matter, but differences in excises.

It is with respect to income taxes – and especially those on income from capital (which includes the corporation tax) – that the most difficult issues will continue to arise. There have already been efforts to impose, as an anti-avoidance device, withholding taxes on interest and dividends that pass across borders, but, mainly because of strong resistance from Britain, this idea has not got very far as yet. Ireland will face increasing pressure over its abnormally low rate of corporation tax and we can expect to see attempts, particularly by those member states between whom labour mobility is reasonably prevalent, to encourage the removal of major differences between personal income taxes.

The idea here is very simple. Would we in Ireland want individual counties to differ in their income taxes? The answer would be negative if we did not want the tax system to influence the location of economic activity within the country. The thrust is now, for certain economic purposes, to regard the EU as a single country (the single market) with individual member states being equivalent to our counties. The concern, therefore, is the way differences in national taxes may influence location.

As to corporation tax, the controversial issues relate to the *effective* rate, which is determined by both the nominal rate and the way the base is defined. The former is politically the more sensitive, but progress is possible, and likely, on the latter. The way taxable profit is determined varies among members, with differences in accounting conventions, depreciation rules, definitions of and restrictions on allowable deductions, the treatment of losses, the treatment of capital gains, provisions relating to transfer pricing, the use of withholding taxes on interest and dividends, and special treatment granted under programmes of investment incentives. Efforts are already being made on these fronts to reduce the differences and we can expect to see these continuing.

On top of this, there are considerable differences in the treatment of dividends, which could influence location. In 2003, of the fifteen member states of the EU, six applied the imputation system, six applied a reduced rate of personal income tax to dividend receipts and two exempted dividends from tax. Ireland was alone in using the classical system, which gives no relief to dividends. However, Ireland is unlikely to experience pressure to move back to the more common European treatment of dividends: the classical system increases the effective tax rate on income from capital and the Commission will probably regard that as a partial quid pro quo for the low nominal rate of corporation tax.

The nominal rate of corporation tax is an example of the political difficulties over tax co-ordination. These difficulties are genuine and cannot be shrugged off. First, tax co-ordination may or may not improve the allocation of resources within the EU as a whole, but what is certain is that, even if it does, any change is likely to have losers as well as gainers. This is, on an international scale, identical to the issue that arises within a country when a tax change is implemented. In this case, the losers are in the same country as the gainers and the problem has to be dealt with internally by whatever fiscal or political mechanism the relevant government chooses to employ (such as compensating losers in some way).

But such mechanisms are much more difficult to bring to bear when the gainers are in different countries from the losers. Thus, the government of a country facing losses (in terms of relative national income as well as domestic revenue) from tax co-ordination will, unless the EU finds some form of compensation, quite properly dig its heels in.

This provides the economic basis for what in EU jargon is called 'subsidiarity': the doctrine that a decision should be made at national level unless there are good reasons for making it at EU level. This can be seen as a reflection of a more fundamental political view – enshrined, for instance, in the federal constitution of the US – that governmental decisions should be made as locally as possible, in the interests of democracy. In the US, taxes are the responsibility of the states unless the constitution gives the power to the federal government, which is why a constitutional amendment was required when the federal income tax was introduced, and will again be required if there is to be a federal sales tax like VAT. The US constitution was written this way in order to induce the smaller states to join the federation – a lesson which has been learned in Europe.

Only if acceptable compensation mechanisms are put in place is there likely to be significant co-ordination of major taxes. To date, the only co-ordination has been in areas where no member state felt that an important interest was at stake, or where the imposition of EU-wide rules required no change by any member state. Examples are minimum general and reduced rates of VAT, minimum excises on certain products, and the treatment of inter-company dividends and capital gains on cross-border transfers of assets. Issues like the corporate tax rate are in a different category.

In the case of VAT, there are likely to be efforts from Brussels to get Ireland to abandon some of the more eccentric features of its current tax, such as the zero-rating of food and children's clothing. This will provide opportunities for posturing, but it is hard to get excited about them. On the one hand, as shown in Chapter 5, these features have little to be said for them and Ireland can hardly claim to lose anything if VAT is applied. On the other hand, the only distortion of the single market arises from cross-border shopping, which is not relevant to Ireland as long as the UK also zero-rates these items.[2]

---

2   There is a complication in that central EU revenue is based on the VAT and so a member state's contribution to the central budget is influenced by that state's VAT structure.

Finally, mention should be made of the argument that tax co-ordination is, even if feasible, not desirable: that is, it is good if member states compete for tax bases by reducing taxes. The point here concerns the size of government. It is claimed that public sectors are inherently less efficient than private sectors and, if revenue is restricted by tax competition, this constrains the size of public sectors and so improves the overall allocation of resources. I will leave you to make up your own mind on this.

Appendix

The Incidence of VAT[1]

THE DISTRIBUTIONAL IMPACT OF NON-UNIFORMITY

An immediate difficulty of non-uniformity is uncertainty (or perhaps ignorance would be a better word) about the pattern of shifting. In general, it is unlikely that an x per cent VAT will increase a price by x per cent: the impact depends on the relative price-elasticities of demand and supply. Given the elasticity of supply, forward shifting is more likely the lower the price-elasticity of demand; and, given the elasticity of demand, shifting is more likely the higher the price-elasticity of supply. Since we do not have enough in the way of detailed estimates of these elasticities, we can only speculate. As a result of the first point, forward shifting is more likely for more 'necessitous' goods and, as a result of the second, it is less likely the more competitive is the structure of supply. In practice, these effects, to some extent anyway, balance out, thus leaving a similar degree of shifting across a wide range of goods and services. Thus, for example, food in general has a relatively low elasticity of demand (encouraging shifting), but its supply is more likely to be in a competitive market structure (discouraging shifting) dominated by supermarkets. On the other hand, less 'necessitous' goods and services have a higher elasticity of demand

---

1 The calculations reviewed here are based on the reduced rate of 12.5 per cent ruling in 2002 rather than the 13.5 per cent rate ruling in 2003. The difference is so trivial (the new rate gives an overall VAT rate only 0.2 percentage points higher than the old rate) that the effect on the results can be ignored, being well within the expected range of error.

(discouraging shifting), but their supply is subject to less competition (encouraging shifting). So, although it is unlikely that VAT in general is fully shifted, the degree of shifting may turn out to be fairly uniform.

In attempting to estimate the incidence of VAT, the first step is to estimate the overall effective rate on the average household consumption basket.[2] Average weekly expenditure for all households in 1999-2000 was £455.47, but we remove the following items: mortgage interest/repayments and residential rentals (included under housing) because it is impossible to estimate the VAT component of these items; motor vehicle duty (included under transport) since this is not consumption but a tax; and donations (included under services and other expenses) since this would involve double-counting. After these adjustments, the tax-inclusive percentage breakdown of the average consumption basket is shown in Table A.1.

Table A.1: Tax-inclusive breakdown of the average household consumption basket (%), 1999-2000

Item	% of total
Food (F)	22.9
Drink and tobacco (DT)	8.6
Clothing and footwear (CF)	6.8
Fuel and light (FL)	4.2
Housing (H)*	2.7
Household non-durables (HND)	2.8
Household durables (HD)	5.2
Miscellaneous goods (MG)	3.8
Transport (T)*	17.6
Services and other expenses (SOE)*	25.3

* see text for adjustments

Using the detailed breakdown shown in the *Household Budget Survey*, each of the categories of consumption in Table A.1 was then divided according to the applicable VAT rate and then the VAT was removed to

2   The basis for this estimate is the figures published in *Household Budget Survey, 1999-2000: Preliminary Results* (Pn 10623, Dublin: Government Publications, 2001).

give the tax-exclusive composition of the consumption of the average household. The results are displayed in Table A.2.

Table A.2: Tax-exclusive breakdown of the average household consumption basket (£ per week), 1999-2000

Item	Total	Exempt	Zero	3%*	12.5%	21%
F	87.54	–	52.02	–	27.38	8.14
DT	28.70	–	–	–	–	28.70
CF	23.77	–	5.27	–	–	18.50
FL	15.28	–	–	–	15.28	–
H	9.95	3.06	–	–	3.76	3.13
HND	9.38	–	–	–	–	9.38
HD	17.48	–	–	–	–	17.48
MG	13.36	–	2.00	–	4.06	7.30
T	63.56	14.14	0.63	12.57	4.34	31.88
SOE	93.61	45.18	4.63	–	2.95	40.85
TOTAL	362.63	62.38	64.55	12.57	57.77	165.36
% of total	*–*	*17.8*	*17.2*	*3.5*	*15.9*	*45.6*

* This is the estimated effective rate applying under the margin scheme for second-hand cars, with the 21 per cent rate applying to a margin assumed to be 15 per cent

Finally, account has to be taken of the fact that, through the imposition of VAT on inputs to exempted final consumption, the effective rate on exempted items is not zero. To estimate this effective rate, use is made of an input-output table.[3] Unfortunately, the input-output table, with only forty-one sectors, is much less detailed than the *Household Budget Survey* that forms the basis of the rest of these estimates. The only three sectors that are approximately coincidental with the exempted consumption items are inland transport, credit and insurance, and non-market health services. From the input-output table, the effective VAT rates are estimated to be

---

3 The most recent available refers to 1993 (*Input-Output Tables 1993*, Pn 7013, Dublin: Government Publications, 1999), but this should not be regarded as a serious difficulty since the input structure of any given output sector should not have changed much in the meantime.

7.1, 3.8, and 8.2 per cent for these sectors respectively. Inland transport is taken as a proxy for exempt passenger transport, credit and insurance aligns well with the exempted banking and insurance, and non-market health services is taken as a proxy for the exempted health and educational services. If the estimated rates are applied to the exempted amounts shown in Table A.2, the weighted average rate for each of the consumption items can be estimated (the weights being the tax exclusive expenditure on each rate category). These estimates are listed in Table A.3.

Table A.3: Weighted average rate (%) of the average household consumption basket, 1999-2000

Item	Average rate
Food (F)	5.9
Drink and tobacco (DT)	21.0
Clothing and footwear (CF)	16.3
Fuel and light (FL)	12.5
Housing (H)	12.5
Household non-durables (HND)	21.0
Household durables (HD)	21.0
Miscellaneous goods (MG)	15.3
Transport (T)	13.6
Services and other expenses (SOE)	11.7
TOTAL	12.5

Thus, the overall effective VAT rate on the average household expenditure basket is estimated to be 12.5 per cent.

This procedure is then repeated for each of the income deciles[4] identified in the *Household Budget Survey*, and the results are displayed in Table A.4.

Thus, with respect to consumption, Ireland's VAT is definitely progressive, though only slightly, with the effective rate increasing by a mere 2.5 percentage points between the first and tenth deciles.

---

4   Decile I refers to the poorest 10 per cent of households, decile II to the next poorest 10 per cent, and so on until decile X, which refers to the richest 10 per cent of households.

Table A.4: Average VAT rates (%) by income decile, 1999-2000

Income decile	Average rate
I	11.0
II	11.1
III	11.4
IV	12.1
V	12.3
VI	12.5
VII	12.6
VIII	12.7
IX	13.1
X	13.5

There is then the more pertinent question of how VAT varies with income. There is a serious problem with the data here in that the disposable income figures in the *Household Budget Survey* are known to be unreliable. However, if we are to make any progress at all, we can do no more than accept those figures.

If we apply the average VAT rates to each decile's consumption, we have the VAT paid by each decile and, if we take that as a percentage of each decile's disposable income, we get the figures shown in Table A.5.

Table A.5 indicates that, across the whole range of household incomes, Ireland's very non-uniform VAT is somewhat regressive with respect to income. However, across the middle eight deciles it is remarkably proportional. Any real regressivity comes solely from the first and tenth deciles. The high rate on the former is accounted for by the fact that total consumption in the poorest decile exceeds by 15 per cent the income of that decile (a result of the fact that this group is dominated by the elderly who typically 'dis-save'). As regards the richest decile, perception is distorted by the fact that this decile is open-ended (it has no upper limit). It could be plausibly speculated that a finer income distribution would show the approximate proportionality of the VAT extending into incomes well above the average income of the ninth decile.

Table A.5: VAT as a percentage of disposable income, 1999-2000

Income decile	VAT as % of disposable income
I	12.2
II	11.1
III	11.2
IV	11.2
V	11.5
VI	11.6
VII	11.1
VIII	10.9
IX	10.5
X	9.1

THE INCIDENCE OF AN ALMOST UNIFORM VAT

The final step is to compare the patterns revealed above with those generated by a VAT that is as uniform as is practicable. By this is meant a tax which zero-rates no household consumption, exempts only banking and insurance,[5] continues to apply the margin scheme to second-hand cars, and applies a single rate to everything else. To be revenue-neutral, such a VAT must have an overall effective rate equal to that of the existing tax – that is, 12.5 per cent. By applying this almost uniform structure to the average household, it is estimated that the required general rate would be 14.1 per cent. If we re-run all our estimates, using this hypothetical structure rather than the existing structure, we obtain the results listed in Table A.6. The regressivity remaining in our simulated VAT is due almost entirely to the exemption of insurance premiums as the proportion of consumption accounted for by this item rises markedly through the deciles.

---

5   Residential rentals would also be exempt, but these have been excluded from our estimates.

Table A.6: Uniform VAT as a percentage of disposable income

Income decile	Average VAT rate %	VAT as % of disposable income
I	13.2	14.7
II	13.1	13.1
III	13.0	12.8
IV	12.9	12.0
V	12.7	11.9
VI	12.6	11.7
VII	12.4	10.9
VIII	12.4	10.5
IX	12.3	9.8
X	12.1	8.1

To aid comparison, Table A.7 sets out the differences between actual and simulated (hypothetical) effective VAT rates and VAT as a percentage of income.

Table A.7: Differences between actual and simulated results

Income decile	Effective VAT rate %	VAT as % of disposable income
I	+2.2	+2.5
II	+2.0	+2.0
III	+1.6	+1.6
IV	+0.8	+0.8
V	+0.4	+0.4
VI	+0.1	+0.1
VII	-0.2	-0.2
VIII	-0.3	-0.4
IX	-0.8	-0.7
X	-1.4	-1.0

The removal of almost all non-uniformity from the VAT certainly makes the tax more regressive, but only slightly so: increasing the liability of the lowest decile by 2.5 percentage points of disposable income and reducing the liability of the highest decile by 1 percentage point of income. However, even this may be an overestimate of the impact because of our assumption that retail prices would all change to the extent of the change in VAT rates. The increased burden on the lower deciles is primarily the effect of the large increase in the rate on food, an item whose distribution is dominated by supermarkets, among which there is intense competition. It would therefore be plausible to speculate that, in practice, an increase in the VAT on food from zero to 14.1 per cent would not cause prices to rise to that extent. It is also plausible to suggest that a reduction in the general rate from 21 to 14.1 per cent would not cause the prices of the relevant goods and services (which are more significant in the budgets of the higher deciles) to decline to that extent, since the degree of competition among suppliers of such items is certainly less than that in the food sector. If these speculations are correct, the increase in regressivity by moving to an almost-uniform VAT would be even less than the estimates indicate.

Further Reading

For those wishing to pursue further the matters discussed in this book, the following should be of help.

The full detail of tax provisions can be found only in the relevant legislation and the regulations supporting it. However, a relatively non-technical, but quite detailed, account of the major provisions can be found in the excellent annual *Taxation Summary* published by the Irish Taxation Institute.

Those with some knowledge of economics who want to know more about the economic analysis of taxation will benefit from the *Tax Policy Handbook* published by the International Monetary Fund (Washington DC, 1995). Very thorough, but somewhat more demanding, is M. P. Devereux (ed.), *The Economics of Tax Policy* (Oxford University Press, 1996). Going yet further involves a major change of gear in terms of economic theory, but the references contained in these two books provide a useful guide. Professional economists will obtain a good idea of modern analysis from G. D. Myles, *Public Economics* (Cambridge University Press, 1995).

The five reports of the Commission on Taxation (Dublin: Government Publications, 1982 to 1985), while dated as regards description, are still of great value as extremely thorough analyses of the issues reviewed in this book.

There has been relatively little research on the economic effects of Irish taxes, but most of what there is can be found in the publications of the Economic and Social Research Institute, Dublin, and in various issues of the *Journal of the Statistical and Social Inquiry Society of Ireland*.

Index

administrative efficiency 31-4, 118
aggregation of income 31-2
agriculture, subsidisation of 94-5
allowances and deductions 44-51
  education and training courses 49-51
  housing 45-8, 117
  medical expenses 48-9, 117
  PAYE credit 42-3, 49, 117
  pension contributions 49, 58-9, 116

benefits in kind 54-5

capital acquisitions tax 90-8
  aggregation of bequests and gifts 90-2
  consanguinity concessions 92-4
  family farms and businesses 94-5
  liquidity issues 95-6
  major issues 92-6
  outline 90-2
  reforms 96
  table 91
  thresholds 90-2, 119
capital allowances 69-71
capital gains tax 4, 25, 28, 33, 66, 76-84
  abolition of indexation 82-3
  accrual versus realisation 77
  bunching 78-9
  capital losses 79, 81
  coverage 79-80
  exemptions 81-2
  gains as income 76-7
  and income tax 37-84
  inflation 78
  Irish 80-4
child benefit 117
children's allowance 53
Commission on Taxation vii
Companies Act 69
concessionary schemes 116-20
corporation tax vii, 2, 37, 66, 72, 119-22

criteria, balancing 34-6
customs duties 120

Denmark social security contributions 2-3
dependants 26
depreciation 69-71, 118
DIRT 34, 60-2, 118
dividends 71-5, 122
donations 50-1

economic approach to tax policy 7-36
  administrative efficiency 31-4
  balancing the criteria 34-6
  horizontal equity 18-28, 34-6, 85, 87,
    88, 118
  progressive, proportional and regressive
    taxes 13-14
  tax incidence 8-13
  vertical equity 29-31, 85, 88, 103, 119
economic efficiency 14-18, 85, 118, 120
  conflict with horizontal equity 34-6
  and excise duty 109-10
  and market mechanisms 14-16
  and PAYE 117
  and wealth tax 88-9
European Central Bank 81
European Commission 62, 108, 121-2
European Economic Community vii
European Union 65, 120-4
excise duty 4, 13-14, 23, 108-13, 120-1
  arguments for 109-11
  economic efficiency 109-10
  Irish 112-13
  issues 109-11
  table 112
  vehicle registration tax 112-13
exempt income 51
  artists and sportspeople 52
  elderly persons 51
  social welfare benefits 52-3

GDP 1-2, 44, 95
globalisation 35
GNP 1-2

home carer's credit 44
horizontal equity 18-28, 85, 118
   conflict with economic efficiency 34-6
   defined 18-19
   definition of the base 24-7
   equal situations 22-8
   equal treatment 28
   special treatment 25-6
   tax unit 19-22
   and wealth tax 87, 88
housing
   effect of stamp duty on cost of 97
   mortgage interest relief 45-8, 117
   rental tax credit 45-8

income tax 4, 17, 37-62
   and administrative efficiency 31-3, 33-4
   aggregation of income 31-2
   allowances and deductions 44-51
   basic structure 39-44,
   benefits in kind 54-5
   and capital gains tax 37-84
   changes in behaviour in response to 12
   company owners 72
   conversion of allowances to credits 39-40
   dissatisfaction with Irish system vii
   and the EU 121-2
   exemptions 33-4, 51-3, 115-18
   global 38-9
   group or individualistic definitions
      19-22, 41-2
   home carer's credit 44
   income-splitting 22
   marginal rates 30
   married couples 20-2, 41-2
   optimal income tax theory 30
   progressive, proportional and regressive
      13-14
   saving and income from saving 55-62
   schedular system 31-2, 38
   self-assessment 33
   sex discrimination 21
   structure 37

and vertical equity 29-30
   see also PAYE
Income Tax Act 69
inflation 78
inheritance tax 90-4
International Financial Services Centre 65

market mechanisms 14-16
married couples 20-2, 41-2
medical expenses 48-9, 117
mortgage interest relief 45-8, 117

OECD 1, 2, 3

PAYE 32, 36
   credits 39, 42-3, 49, 58-9, 117
   economic efficiency 117
   employer's role 32-3
pensions 49, 57-9, 116
property tax 12-13, 47, 89, 118, 119
   see also wealth tax
PRSI 62-5

rental tax credit 45-8

saving 86, 94, 118
   DIRT 34, 60-2, 118
   and income from saving 55-62
   pension schemes 57-9
   SSIAs 60
Schedule A 45-7
Schedule C 38
Schedule D 38, 65
Schedule E 38-9, 42, 52
Schedule F 72
self-assessment 33, 88-9
Shannon Airport 65
social welfare contributions 2-4, 38, 59,
   62-5
stamp duty 4, 12, 89, 96-8

tables
   Average VAT rates by income decile
      129
   CAT thresholds 91
   Differences between actual and
      simulated results (VAT) 131

Excise as a % of retail price 112
Net tax revenue by type of base 6
Net tax revenue by type of tax 5
Rates of social welfare contribution for
    Class A employees 63
Revenue foregone by selected reliefs
    116
Selected effective rates of income tax
    42
Selected tax credits 40
Standard rate brackets 41
Structure of tax revenue 3
Tax saving with two earners 43
Tax-exclusive breakdown of the
    average household consumption
    basket 127
Tax-inclusive breakdown of the average
    household consumption basket 126
Total tax revenue 1
Uniform VAT as a % of disposable
    income 131
VAT as a % of disposable income 130
Weighted average rate of the average
    household consumption basket 128
tax capitalisation 12-13
tax evasion 34, 36, 61-2, 89, 120
tax incidence 8-13
tax period 23-4
tax policy vii
    economic approach 7-36
tax reform vii, 96
tax unit 19-22
taxation
    concessions 115-16
    current system 115-24
    double 87-8
    the future 120-4
    lack of neutrality 115
    non-uniformity and complexity 119-20
    overview of Irish system 1-6
    reliefs 116-17
    structure of tax revenue 1-6
taxation of profits 65-76
    capital allowances 69-71
    close companies 75
    dividends 71-5
    example of Irish subsidiary 67-8

tax rates 65-9
    transfer pricing 75-6
third-level and training courses 49-50

UK social security contributions 2-4
US tax system 67, 72, 123

VAT 4, 13-14, 16-17, 23, 99-108, 120-1
    and administrative efficiency 33
    basis of 99-101
    consumption versus production 101
    differential rates 30-1
    and equal treatment 28
    exemption 102, 104
    and housing 97-8, 105-6
    impact on behaviour 9-12
    incidence of an almost uniform 130-2
    incidence of Irish 107-8
    major features in Ireland 104-8
    non-uniformity 106-7, 119, 125-30
    origin versus destination principle 101-2
    as a percentage of disposable income
        130
    rates 103-5
    self-assessment 33, 101
    tables 126-31
    three methods 99-100
    turnover threshold 100, 104
    zero-rating 102-5, 121, 123
vehicle registration tax 112, 113
vertical equity 29-31, 85
    defined 29
    and economic efficiency 29
    and income tax 29-30
    and VAT 103, 119
    and wealth tax 88

wealth tax 13, 85-98, 119
    definition of wealth 86-7
    and double taxation 87-8
    practical difficulties 88-9
    reasons for 86, 88
    see also property tax
withholding tax 32
    DIRT 34, 60-2, 118
    see also PAYE
World Trade Organisation 120